David Foster Wallace's
Infinite Jest

CONTINUUM CONTEMPORARIES

Also available in this series:

Forthcoming in this series:

· DAVID FOSTER WALLACE'S

Infinite
Jest

A READER'S GUIDE

STEPHEN BURN

CONTINUUM | NEW YORK | LONDON

2011

Continuum International Publishing Group
80 Maiden Lane, Suite 704, New York, NY 10038
The Tower Building, 11 York Road, London SE1 7NX

www.continuumbooks.com

Library of Congress Cataloging-in-Publication Data

Burn, Stephen.
    David Foster Wallace's Infinite jest : a reader's guide / Stephen Burn.
        p. cm. — (Continuum contemporaries)
    Includes bibliographical references.
    ISBN 0-8264-1477-X (pbk. : alk. paper)
    1. Wallace, David Foster. Infinite jest.   I. Title: Infinite jest.   II. Title.   III. Series.
PS3573.A42563515433   2003
813'.54—dc21   2003003733

ISBN 978-08264-1477-9

Printed and bound in the United States of America

Contents

To my parents.

Acknowledgements

Lesley and Russ Burn; Jon Adams; Audrey, Denis and Sophie Ferguson; Patricia Waugh; Pete Dempsey; David Myles; David Barker; and especially Julie: sorry all over the place.

1

The Novelist

"KINDS OF PAIN" (p. 987n24)

How difficult does literature need to be? At what point does the obscurity or complexity of a novel render the vast rewards it may offer irrelevant? Looking back from century's end, these two questions seem to be the haunting anxieties of twentieth-century fiction. So many of the most respected books of the last hundred years are so forbiddingly esoteric, syntactically dense, and formally complex, that they seem accessible only to the most dedicated and initiated readers. But why (in a century that was otherwise amusing itself to death) should this be the case? In a recent essay for the *New Yorker* Jonathan Franzen argued that this situation was a result of critics and readers confusing their categories, allowing impenetrability to shade into literary quality, until the two seem indivisible. Writers like James Joyce, William Gaddis, and Robert Musil, Franzen argued, had been misled by this blurring of categories, and had become "status" authors: writers who disdained the reader and saw the difficulty of their novels as a proof of their intellectual achievement.

In a follow-up interview with the same magazine, Franzen was asked whether David Foster Wallace's massive novel, *Infinite Jest*, was a product of the same disconnection between entertainment-seeking reader and expert writer. The question was almost inevitable because, since it was published in 1996, Wallace's novel has become a kind of exemplar for difficulty in contemporary fiction. Even on the shelves of bookstores it seems an intimidating proposition, its 1079 dense pages dwarfing surrounding volumes by Walker and Waugh. But largeness alone is not the only difficulty facing the reader of *Infinite Jest*. The verbal invention and length of Wallace's sentences, the gaps and loops in the novel's chronology, and the obliqueness of much of the narration, mean that even after a couple of readings such a basic question as "what happened?" is still difficult to resolve.

In spite of these difficulties, however, Franzen categorized *Infinite Jest* as the work of a "contract," rather than a "status," author. According to Franzen's model, *Infinite Jest* is a work whose main aim was pleasure and connection. It establishes a compact with readers, relying on their faith that its author's aim is to entertain rather than test them; and its difficulties, Franzen contends, do not extend beyond its formidable length. But while he is undoubtedly right to draw attention to how entertaining Wallace's work is, his unequivocal description of *Infinite Jest* as a contract novel hints at a certain lack of integrity to Franzen's categories. Wallace's novel is surely no easier to read than some status novels that Franzen discards, like Gaddis's *A Frolic of His Own* (1994). And, in fact, a fuller understanding of *Infinite Jest* to some extent depends upon recognizing that the novel *does* place demands upon the reader, and then trying to work out why. The reasons turn out to be organically connected to what the novel is trying to say about entertainment, and are, to some extent, entangled in a series of literary, historical, and personal issues that include the novel's relation to earlier works, and Wallace's personal history as a reader. But to appreciate this, it is first necessary to know a little more about Wallace's background and his other books.

David Foster Wallace was born in Ithaca, New York, in 1962 to James Donald (a philosophy Professor) and Sally Wallace (an English teacher). They were living in upstate New York at least partly because his father had completed a Ph.D. in the area, but the family relocated to the Midwest when Wallace was still young. They moved to Philo, Illinois, which Wallace has described in a semi-autobiographical essay as "a tiny collection of corn silos and war-era Levittown homes whose native residents did little but sell crop insurance and nitrogen fertilizer and herbicide and collect property taxes" (*Fun*, p. 3). Amid the grid of Illinois farmland, Wallace displayed an early talent for tennis (he reports that at age fourteen he was ranked seventeenth in the region) but his later successes as a student made it clear that Wallace's talents were more cerebral than athletic; he graduated *summa cum laude* in 1985 from Amherst College in Massachusetts, received an MFA in Creative Writing from the University of Arizona, and then did graduate work in Philosophy at Harvard. But what this transcript partly disguises is the unusual versatility of Wallace's intellectual development. As Wallace explained in an interview with Larry McCaffery, his academic career traced an unconventional shift from algorithms to fiction:

For most of my college career I was a hard-core syntax wienie, a philosophy major with a specialization in math and logic. . . . I was just awfully good at technical philosophy, and it was the first thing I'd ever been really good at, and so everybody, including me, anticipated I'd make it a career. But it sort of emptied out for me somewhere around age twenty. . . . So what I did, I went back home for a term, planning to play solitaire and stare out the window, whatever you do in a crisis. And all of a sudden I found myself writing fiction. (pp. 138–39)

But if Wallace's pastimes, chasing the mathematical satisfactions of proof completion and playing tennis, seem unlikely stepping stones toward writing fiction, it is notable that they have both clearly fed into his work. Tennis is one of the major subjects of *Infinite Jest*, while his interest in math logic presumably accounts for the insistence on precision and technical detail that often characterizes his prose. And the broad outlines of the rest of Wallace's biography seem to suggest a straightforward correspondence between his life and his writing. Powerful, intellectually gifted parents loom large in his fiction, while the geography of his later life is retraced in his writing, with *Infinite Jest* in particular replaying Wallace's crossings between Arizona and Massachusetts. And even the kind of emptiness in high talent that Wallace found at the end of his mathematical career, seems to be recalled in Hal's anhedonia in *Infinite Jest*.

It may seem tempting, then, to move from this account to a more detailed interpretation of Wallace's novel, trying to find a biographical pattern that explains why *Infinite Jest*, with its manipulative mother and distant father, offers a mirror image of the marginal mother and darkly ubiquitous father of *The Broom of the System* (1987). But Wallace would presumably agree with Amherst's Emily Dickinson, when she wrote that "Biography first convinces us of the fleeing of the Biographied" (p. 864), because he has already noted how he has attempted to thwart such readings by reversing the genders in his first book. And, in fact, the more we learn about Wallace the *less* helpful a biographical reading of *Infinite Jest* seems to be.

Wallace's essay "Derivative Sport in Tornado Alley" offers an instructive example in this context because its mixture of apparent autobiography, tennis, and mathematics initially seems so promising. As some reviewers of *Infinite Jest* noted, the essay contains tempting clues, but to try and map this life sketch onto the novel quickly results in frustration. For example, Wallace describes himself in the essay as a "near-great" tennis player (p. 3), a self-description that

Hal's grandfather assumes (p. 158). If this hints, though, that the novel should be read according to a Wallace ⇔ James Incandenza senior correspondence, this simple equation is soon complicated because Wallace also describes himself in terms of his profuse over-sweating, a characteristic that suggests that his true counterpart may be *Infinite Jest*'s sweaty Marlon Bain. And even the names in the essay tend to complicate, rather than resolve, interpretations of the novel. One of Wallace's apparently real acquaintances, for example, shares the surname "Lord" with *Infinite Jest*'s Otis P. Lord, but trying to trace this name seems to lead to Emily Dickinson's biography rather than Wallace's, as Otis P. Lord was a Salem judge whom Dickinson seems to have been in love with. It may be possible to unravel the connections between Wallace's life and fiction in the future, but it seems better to conclude now that Wallace's past and personality are freely diffused throughout the whole book, with any pattern being (as yet) unlocatable.

But if, in general, it is wiser not to try to interpret the book through the lens of Wallace's past, one biographical strand that seems crucial to understanding both *Infinite Jest*'s take on entertainment, and the demands it places upon the reader, is Wallace's relation to the preceding generation of postmodern American writers. It is not for nothing that reviewers of *Infinite Jest* have tended to approach the work from this perspective, seeing Wallace as the gifted offspring of "Pop Pynchon" (LeClair, "Radical Realism," p. 16), or as "a student of literary post-modernists like John Barth and Robert Coover" (McInerney, p. 8), because Wallace's fiction is clearly both inspired by, and an attempt to progress beyond, postmodernism's endgame.

Wallace even dates his origin as a writer from his experience reading Donald Barthelme's "The Balloon," but the impact of this kind of metafiction clearly went beyond simply inspiring Wallace's apprentice work. A lingering influence can be detected even in the late-1990s where the brief interviews that punctuate Wallace's writing read like one-sided variations of Barthelme stories like "The Explanation." And, in fact, Wallace's response to his postmodern ancestors can be seen to be a unifying thread throughout his fiction.

I have argued elsewhere (see "Generational Succession") that the title of Wallace's first novel deliberately echoes a passage from De-Lillo's *Americana* (1971), and despite its originality *The Broom of the System* also includes other links backwards: as many reviewers noted, the skeleton of its plot echoes Oedipa Maas's strange bequest from Pierce Inverarity in Pynchon's *The Crying of Lot 49* (1966); the stretches of unattributed dialogue in the work recall Gaddis's dialogue-driven novels; and the receptionist Candy Mandible (despite being an obvious pun), perhaps owes her name to the teacher in Barthelme's short story "Me and Miss Mandible."

The stories collected in *Girl With Curious Hair* (1989) extend this network of allusions with references to Cynthia Ozick, Joseph McElroy, and Barthelme, but it is the final story, "Westward the Course of Empire Takes its Way," that represents an ambivalent zenith. The collection's copyright page describes this story as "written in the margins of John Barth's 'Lost in the Funhouse,'" and it relates the attempts of a very thinly-veiled caricature of Barth to open a "Funhouse" chain of restaurants. Wallace told Larry McCaffery that the story was an attempt to "do with metafiction what . . . DeLillo's *Libra* had done with other mediated myths . . . I wanted to get the Armageddon-explosion, the goal metafiction's always been about, I wanted to get it over with, and then out of the rubble reaffirm the idea of art being a living transaction between humans" (p. 142). However, while the story succeeds as a humorous account of the commodification of self-reflexive postmodernism, as an attempt to expose the illusions of metafiction by a kind of meta-metafiction, the work becomes tangled in its own recursive spiral.

While *Infinite Jest* is not without its own elaborate structure of references to postmodern ancestors (one character, for example, raids Pynchon's work to steal Pig Bodine's surname as a pseudonym, and defends it as "a private chuckle" [p. 1014n110]), its approach is somewhat different to the recursion of "Westward." There is a seven-year gap between *Girl With Curious Hair* and *Infinite Jest* and in that period Wallace decided (somewhat harshly) that "Westward" was "a permanent migraine" ("Interview," p. 142), a guide of what not to do, although his goal of human connection remained the same. This change in attitude is revealed in the essays that Wallace wrote while he was composing the later novel, in which his obsession with the limits of postmodernism is distilled in its purest form. The crucial text here is Wallace's essay, "E Unibus Pluram: Television and U.S. Fiction," which offers an anatomy of post-war American fiction's ambivalent relationship with television, and a prescription for new fiction.

The early cultural impact of television had been registered by a number of writers at midcentury. In 1950 T.S. Eliot wrote to the *Times* with reactionary concerns about the "effect (mentally, morally, and physically)" mass spectation could have (p. 7), while five years later, in *The Recognitions*, Gaddis had presciently begun to outline how the world was changing to one where "images surround us" (p. 152). From Wallace's perspective nearer the millennium, however, the salient facts about television were its emphasis on surface, and its adoption of self-referring postmodern irony as a form of self-defense.

The first of these strands develops from television's need to maintain a fairly accurate finger on the pulse of national desire so that it can serve up what people want, and ensure as much watching as possible. It naturally becomes clear, from this, that attractive people are more pleasant to watch, particularly if these pretty people are "*geniuses* at seeming unwatched" (p. 25), unaffected by the kind of inner doubt and self-consciousness that afflicts most people faced by an audience. And because television typically presents lives that seem more perfect than our own, these pretty watchable people are idealized, and every time the viewer turns on the television they receive "unconscious reinforcement of the deep thesis that the most significant quality of truly alive persons is watchableness" (p. 26).

This leads Wallace to speculate on the impact of so much spectation upon the viewer's sense of self. If the most highly prized personal attribute is a watchable exterior, and the lonely viewer has begun to view a relationship with characters portrayed in "television's 2-D images" (p. 38) as an acceptable alternative to connecting with "real 3-D persons" (p. 39), then human identity becomes "vastly more spectatorial" (p. 34), located in shallow surfaces, and exteriors. This, however, is obviously an empty and emotionally impoverished existence. But TV needs to ensure more watching, so to prevent viewers from realizing its role in their unhappiness, it has, since the 1980s, become increasingly self-referential, presenting television shows about television shows. By making the viewer watch shows about watching, TV aims to delude viewers into thinking that they are intellectually critiquing spectation, rather than passively consuming. And it is here, Wallace contends, that television's connection with postmodern literature lies, because these strategies have been drawn from contemporary fiction. Television shows now adopt the ironic humor of much metafiction, and begin to poke fun at themselves, and dramatize their limitations. By wryly encouraging the viewer to "eat a whole lot of food and stare at the TV" (p. 41), the illusion is fostered that a passivity that has only been acknowledged has actually been transcended. Wallace summarizes: "it is now *television* that takes elements of the *postmodern*—the involution, the absurdity, the sardonic fatigue, the iconoclasm and rebellion—and bends them to the ends of spectation and consumption" (p. 64).

Alongside this account of television, Wallace traces three evolutions in the way American fiction has responded since the 1960s. The first wave of postmodern literature that engaged with pop culture included the early works of Gaddis, Barth, and Pynchon, who found television-images valid objects of literary allusion. But television was of more importance to writers who emerged in the 1970s and 1980s and located their purpose "in its commentary on/response to a U.S. culture more and more of and for watching, illusion, and the video image" (Ibid.). For these first two generations irony was a ground-clearing tool wielded with the idealist belief that "etiology and diagnosis pointed toward cure, that a revelation of imprisonment led to freedom" (p. 67). It is, however, the third group and the work they produce (which he calls "Image Fiction"), that concerns Wallace.

These writers (such as A.M. Homes, William Vollmann, and Mark Leyner) are distinct from the previous generations because their work is not simply using televisual culture, but attempting to respond to it, attempting to restore the television-flattened world "to three whole dimensions" (p. 52). But, according to Wallace, this attempt fails because the new writers rely on the tools of their postmodern precursors: an irony that television has already absorbed, and now uses to its own advantage. And Image Fiction degenerates to the superficiality of the shows they try to expose, "doomed to shallowness by its desire to ridicule a TV-culture whose mockery of itself and all value already absorbs all ridicule" (p. 81). The only way forward, for Wallace, is to effect a break with postmodern practice, and abandon protective irony and risk sincerity. He concludes:

The next real literary "rebels" in this country might well emerge as some weird bunch of *anti*-rebels . . . who dare somehow to back away from ironic watching, who have the childish gall actually to . . . treat of plain old untrendy human troubles and emotions in U.S. life with reverence and conviction. Who eschew self-consciousness . . . The new rebels might be artists willing to risk the yawn, the rolled eyes, the cool smile, the nudged rubs, the parody of gifted ironists. (p. 81)

This rejection of irony, and the televisual culture it has become synonymous with, has important consequences for the way character is perceived in fiction. Wallace's essay describes a progressive flattening of the self in a culture defined by electronic wave and signal. A loss of depth, that is reinscribed in the surface mimesis of Image Fiction. And Wallace argues that such fictions are diminishing the role fiction can fulfill. He told McCaffery:

If you operate, which most of us do, from the premise that there are things about the contemporary U.S. that make it distinctively hard to be a real human being, then maybe half of fiction's job is to dramatize what it is that makes it tough. The other half is to dramatize the fact that we still *are* human beings, now. Or can be. ("Interview," p. 131)

This is an important statement of Wallace's critique of much contemporary fiction, and an implicit outline of *Infinite Jest*'s project. In the next chapter I detail how the novel makes this struggle to escape two-dimensionality and achieve fuller selfhood one of its central explorations, but Wallace's account of a nation in front of the television also has other large consequences for *Infinite Jest*.

If contemporary culture presents a bewildering range of passive entertainments that foster a shallowness of self, then Wallace responds by making his novel resist passive consumption. Although an author-surrogate in *Infinite Jest* announces that "his most serious wish was: *to entertain*" (p. 839), the novel complicates its appeal by deliberately making demands on the reader with its vast size, encyclopedic knowledge, and elusive plot. As it does so, it suggests more revealing continuities and divergences from both postmodernist and modernist works.

Infinite Jest's encyclopedic form most clearly recalls the tradition of massive fictions written by older postmodernists that began with Gaddis's *The Recognitions,* and includes later works like Thomas Pynchon's *Gravity's Rainbow* (1973), Gaddis's second novel, *JR* (1975), and Don DeLillo's *Underworld* (1997). The writers of such works would presumably agree with Pynchon's observation that "since 1959, we have come to live among flows of data more vast than anything the world has seen before" ("Luddite," p. 1), because the form and content of their works both present and are shaped by an information-dense world. Joseph McElroy's vast *Women and Men* (1987), for example, registers an "awesome excess of data" (p. 1112), while even the aesthetically-suffused consciousness of William Kohler (who narrates William Gass's *The Tunnel* [1995]) seems to recognize this contemporary fact, as he wryly reflects that he was "made wretchedly ill . . . by raw data" (p. 51).

But behind their postmodern data collection are Joyce's *Ulysses* (1922), which he described as "a kind of encyclopaedia" (*Selected Letters,* p 271), and the "unfallable encyclicling" (p. 153.26) of *Finnegans Wake* (1939). Like the later postmodern works, Joyce's novels make an attempt at "containing the encyclopedia" (*Ulysses,* p. 838), and their obsession with data seems to have a specific goal, as *Ulysses's* example, in particular, demonstrates.

Written through the years 1914–1922, *Ulysses* is an encyclopedia stored up against the possible destruction of western civilization by world war. It is designed, as Joyce explained, to contain "a picture of Dublin so complete that if the city one day suddenly disappeared from the earth it could be reconstructed out of my book" (Budgen, p. 69). Although rarely recognized, this idea is one of the essential foundations of the book, as Bloomsday (with its more than incidental suggestion of doomsday) is strategically set on the brink of apocalypse. "Tomorrow," Leopold Bloom reflects, "is killing day" (p. 122), and although on a literal level this refers to the city's abattoirs, the darker reference is to the sound of falling cities, "shattered glass and toppling masonry" (pp. 28, 54, 683), that echoes throughout the novel.

Written in what may have seemed equally dark times, the ency-clopedic novels of post-atomic America seem to share this aim. *Gravity's Rainbow* concludes on the brink of a nuclear winter, but it moves against devastation by storing the marginalized voices of many continents. In the more private apocalypse of *The Recogni-tions*, which details both art and the self's erasure in its double end-ing, it is artistic history that is stored by Gaddis's survey. These novels are, like *Ulysses*, vast cultural data banks created in the face of the planet's ruin.

The encyclopedic project of *Infinite Jest*, with its detailed "data-retrieval" (p. 322), overlaps, to some extent, with this model. It is, after all, notable that it is postmodern encyclopedists like Gaddis that Wallace sees of most value amongst older postmodernists, al-though Joyce is an unmistakably important influence (not only does the novel twice repeat Buck Mulligan's word "scrotum-tightening" [pp. 112, 605], and share *Ulysses's* interest in "telemachry" [p. 249], but the clearest allusion of all is surely that the novel is stalked by the ghost of a tall alcoholic author named Jim). And it is surely also significant that (as I explain in the next chapter) the chronology of Wallace's novel begins in 1960, at the start of the age in which Pyn-chon had diagnosed data as the significant contemporary fact.

But while Wallace extends their work, at the same time he cri-tiques this obsession with encyclopedic knowledge. If, as Tom LeClair has argued, writers like Pynchon, Gaddis, and McElroy saw their gathering of information as a positive project, an attempt to counter the mass media's "thin layer of superficial information" with their profound and dense data (*The Art of Excess*, p. 16), *Infinite Jest* dramatizes the limitations of this attempt. Its fundamental process is to seek exhaustive accounts, and to dramatize the accumulation of information, but most of these efforts (like Hal's attempt to list everything blue in the headmaster's waiting room [p. 508]) prove empty and futile exercises. Several examples of this are explored in more detail in the next chapter, but two of the most obvious feature Gately's stepfather and Steeply's father.

These characters are both obsessed with "data analysis" (p. 507), but in each case Wallace shows their cataloging to be indicative of a deeper lack of control. Gately's stepfather, for example, is a vicious alcoholic, who precisely records every drink he has in his notebook. He is, Wallace explains, "the sort of person who equated incredibly careful record-keeping with control" (p. 841), but after eight drinks he inevitably begins to beat his wife according to a "regular schedule" (p. 446).

The cruelty of Steeply's father, by contrast, is more emotional, as he shuts out his family so that he can catalog insane details from the television show he is addicted to. As he is gradually consumed by this obsession, he increasingly gives his time to the "scrupulous recording of tiny details, in careful order" (p. 641), and developing "baroque systems of cross-reference" (p. 642), but loses his job and his sanity.

It is, of course, not coincidental that these destructive characters are both addicts. Encyclopedic data storage is, for Wallace, another potentially dangerous addiction, and their attempt to control data leads to larger slippages in their lives. Wallace sets against them his more positive characters, like Mario and Lyle, who "take data pretty much as it comes" (p. 379). They may seem to know less, but they are in many ways more alive than the other "data-entry drone[s]" (p. 910).

There is something similar in William Vollmann's *You Bright and Risen Angels* (1987), which mocks the desire for inclusivity by incorporating a detailed list of contents for a second volume that does not exist, and features (as one of its two narrators) a writer who admits that "this is a bookish novel because I, the author, know little of life" (p. 595). But perhaps a more revealing comparison comes from a nineteenth-century writer. In his essay "Circles," Emerson insisted that "all the argument and all the wisdom is not in the encyclopædia" (p. 111), and *Infinite Jest*'s survey suggests that Wallace would agree with this. The roots of the term *encyclopedia* lie in a misreading of the Greek *enkýlios paideíá*, and denote the circle of learning, but the many circles in *Infinite Jest* (the "circular routine" of addiction [p. 53], the *"circle of . . . retribution"* [p. 713]), bring little real knowledge. This is even stressed by the largest circle of all, the book itself. As the narrative approaches its inconclusive final stages Wallace, in a metafictional remark, observes that it is moving "toward what's either a climax or the end of the disk" (p. 807). But as the reader who reaches page 981 realizes, the final pages are not really the climax (Wallace has already related the novel's end on page 886), but an invitation to circle back to the beginning of the narrative disk to review the crucial information from the Year of Glad. And Emerson's message is underlined because completing this circle of learning from the novel still leaves the reader's knowledge incomplete. Part of Wallace's aim seems to be to break with self-reference and direct the reader outside of the book, to find what has escaped the encyclopedia, and indirectly underline James Fenimore Cooper's observation in *The Pathfinder* (1840): "much book, little know" (p. 12).

2

The Novel

"(AT LEAST) THREE CHEERS FOR CAUSE AND EFFECT"
(p. 991n24)

About a third of the way through *Infinite Jest*, the crisis point in one of the novel's multiple narrative lines comes as an elaborate war game, played out with a mixture of old tennis equipment and calculus, descends into a dispute over the relationship between the game's boundaries and the imagined territory they represent. As November snow begins to fall, one of the younger players, J. J. Penn, claims that the cold weather will restrict the damage his nation has taken in the game, but this challenge to the game's founding principle infuriates Michael Pemulis. "It's snowing on the goddamn *map*, not the *territory*" (p. 333), he yells. Others join in the argument, questioning "is the territory the real world, quote unquote, though" (p. 334), and the game falls away from its "elegant complexity" (p. 322) into an all-out brawl.

This is a key scene because the ensuing scuffle instigates a number of chains of cause and effect that lead into the novel's climactic last days, but it is also significant because it illustrates the complications that can emerge from trying to map a larger world, an important concern when setting out to map such a difficult book. A map, as Pemulis realizes, is subject to all kinds of distortions and local disturbances that may have no relation to the complex topographies of the territory. And, as Wallace shows, the two can easily be confused, leading to chaotic consequences. But is it possible for some sort of perfect map to escape these limitations? To try and answer this, it is revealing to read Wallace's scene alongside Jorge Luis Borges's parable of mapmaking, "Of Exactitude in Science." In Borges's postmodern fable the cartographers of the Empire achieve such a level of perfection in their craft that the map of the Empire eventually reaches the same scale as the Empire itself. Map and territory coincide point for point. But if this suggests that one solution to the young players' confusion would be to have a map of comparable scale (where the map coexists with the territory the distinction becomes a moot point), the end of Borges's sketch offers a warning. Such a large map of the Empire inevitably becomes ridiculously cumbersome to later generations, and is abandoned to the weather that Wallace's players are arguing about in the first place: "the Rigours of sun and Rain" (p. 131) destroy the map and eventually the entire discipline of Geography disappears from the nation.

The lessons of Borges's parable, though, apply not only to this scene, but also to the outline of the novel that this book offers. Although like all maps, this short guide inevitably runs the risk that readers may confuse map and territory, it is important to recognize that because *Infinite Jest* depends on the reader reconstructing a larger narrative from a number of subtle hints and apparently incidental details, a sufficiently detailed map of the novel would (in contrast to Borges's map of Empire) probably be even larger than the intimidating 1079 page terrain that already makes up the work. While such a plan is obviously not feasible, without some help the reader faced with the novel's tangled narrative lines and scattered chronology may feel like they need the sort of "genius for navigating cluttered fields" (p. 141) that Hal ascribes to the postmodern hero. This has apparently even been the case for professional readers. As the survey of the novel's reception in chapter three shows, reviewers (perhaps understandably struggling against deadlines with such a long and complex book) made both factual and interpretative errors. And even so perceptive a reader as Frederick Karl has noted that, in the face of *Infinite Jest*'s narrative looping, "a reader's guide to the novel would be helpful" (p. 473).

But if *Infinite Jest* eludes total mapping, a small guide to this big novel is still possible because the larger outlines of the structure and chronology of Wallace's novel are themselves quite suggestive. As this is the first book to be devoted to Wallace's fiction, however, the sane cartographer has to recognize that his map will necessarily be partial, and that the collaborative work of later mapmakers will add detail and revise the terrain. In providing this outline, though, I hope to show that, as Hal argues, "the map speaks for itself" (p 1017n110).

As the snow falls on the Eschaton map in *Infinite Jest*, the narrator describes how the change in weather has eliminated "all visual background so that the map's action seems stark and surreal" (p. 341). To begin to map the novel itself a similar strategy is necessary. The reader has to refine much of the novel's complex plot out of their field of vision to perceive the larger skeleton of the work.

Having done this, the first markers to place down locate the novel's temporal boundaries. But because Wallace is presenting a corporate America where even calendar years are auctioned-off and renamed after the highest bidder (so, one of the novel's most important years is the "Year of the Depend Adult Undergarment," with the advertising bonus of a nappy-wearing Statue of Liberty) this is not as easy as it might seem. Although on page 223 Wallace offers a chronology of the nine years of "subsidized time," the date that this sponsorship began is never explicitly given in the text.

Faced with this uncertainty, most reviewers and critics of *Infinite Jest* have speculated about the precise dating of the novel's action. In Tom LeClair's informative essay, for example, the novel's action is located at "about 2015" ("Prodigious Fiction," p. 31), while Steve Brzezinski, reviewing the book for the *Antioch Review*, sets the date a year earlier, at "2014" (p. 491). Other readers like Dale Peck, how-ever, have instead insisted that "it's impossible to pin down when exactly" the action takes place (p. 14). In spite of Peck's claim, though, it is possible to precisely date the action, but to do so it is necessary to cross-reference two endnotes referring to the fictional M.I.T. Language Riots.

These riots (which, given that they occur in DeLillo's *Ratner's Star* [p. 31], are presumably meant as a subtle intertextual joke) are first mentioned in Wallace's novel as having taken place in "1997" (p. 987n24). A little later in the novel, in a section from the Year of the Depend Adult Undergarment (abbreviated in the novel to Y.D.A.U.), an endnote refers to "the so-called M.I.T. Language Riots of twelve years past" (p. 996n60). From this we can deduce that Y.D.A.U., the eighth year of subsidized time, is 2009. Subsidiza-tion therefore began in 2002, and the latest action in the novel, which takes place in the Year of Glad, can be dated as 2010.

Although characters recall events from further back (such as the career-ending knee injury which James Incandenza's father suffered in 1933), the earliest action which is dramatized in the novel is from 1960 (on pages 157–69), so the temporal brackets of the novel can be set around a fifty-year period extending from 1960 to 2010. Hav-ing established the chronological limits of the work, the next step is to try to understand the structure of the work in which this chronol-ogy unfolds. This is again important because so many readers of the work have found *Infinite Jest* diffuse, and random. Michiko Kakutani, for example, in her review of the novel for the *New York Times Book Review*, sums up this perspective when she describes the compositional principle of the work as nothing more than a "compendium of whatever seems to have crossed Mr. Wallace's mind" (p. B2). However, while *Infinite Jest* may not be divided into conventional chapters, and often abruptly shifts focus between paragraphs, the text is still broken up, and it is done so with much more care than readers like Kakutani have assumed. In fact, the divisions in the text are of more than usual importance because they allow Wallace to signal to the reader that the novel is about to shift between narrative lines, or between locations, or to move forwards or backwards in time.

Wallace uses three distinct methods to mark these divisions in his text. The first way he signals a break is by a capitalized heading which is either a date or a title. The second is by the resumption of a narrative after a clear break (such as on page 666 after a letter, or on page 787 where an endnote intrudes). And the third is by the insertion of one of the 28 circles that interrupt the main text. Applying these divisions strictly, the novel turns out to be composed of ninety individual sections.

Now if the novel, as I suggested in the last chapter, partly explores the encyclopedic urge to understand, measure, and categorize, then numerology is certainly one of its procedures, and it makes sense to search for some deeper significance that would explain Wallace's choice of the number 90. One of the most suggestive occurrences of the number is revealed toward the end of the book, when the ghost of James Incandenza explains that he "spent the whole sober last ninety days of his animate life" (p. 838) creating the film *Infinite Jest*. So the structure of the novel, far from being random, seems to be subtly arranged to parallel the composition of the film that it is about.

But if viewing the book at this "macrocartographic scale" (p. 1032n176) reveals how surprisingly controlled the architecture of *Infinite Jest* is, it is necessary to return to the more confusing human scale in order to begin disentangling the plot's lines of cause and effect. At this scale we are faced with what Frederick Karl calls "an unsolvable, virtually impenetrable world of behavior" (p. 473), and ambiguity and doubt seem to surround most of the important events. It is possible, though, to disentangle (at least) three major plot lines that unfold in Y.D.A.U.

The first narrative the reader is introduced to concentrates on Hal Incandenza, a richly talented student at the Enfield Tennis Academy (E.T.A.) in Massachusetts, who is seventeen years old in Y.D.A.U. Hal is the son of the extravagantly gifted physicist, tennis-mind, and filmmaker James Orin Incandenza, and has inherited (amongst other bequests) an addictive personality from his father. By November Y.D.A.U. he has been secretly getting high every day for over a year, and has now begun to agonizingly withdraw from marijuana.

In one of the novel's many dark symmetries, Hal's decline and withdrawal is inverted in the second narrative which traces the recovery of former burglar Don Gately from his Demerol and Talwin addiction at Ennet House, a halfway house that is literally and metaphorically down the hill from E.T.A. In November Y.D.A.U., 29 year-old Gately has been completely substance free for more than a year, but as he lies wounded in a hospital he may be on the brink of accepting Demerol once again.

Entangled in these two narratives is a larger political plot. The last work Hal's father completed was *Infinite Jest*, a film so compelling that the spectator is willing to pass up all necessary sustenance in favor of watching the film again and again, and entertaining themselves to death. The third narrative details the race between Québecois separatists and American agents to gain a master copy of this film, with the separatists aiming to circulate the film to allow the American audience to fatally indulge their love of spectation, thus fracturing diplomatic relations between the United States and Canada.

Separating the narrative out into three strands like this, however, produces a deceptively straightforward map of the work, and the novel quite explicitly resists this kind of reduction, asking "are you just looking for some Cliff-Note summary so you can incorporate the impression of depth into some new panty-removal campaign?" (p. 1012n110). Instead, the complex interactions of the novel's plot have more in common with the rejection of linear narrative in some of the most sophisticated post-war novels. Although *Gravity's Rainbow* acknowledges that the reader "will want cause and effect" (p. 663), Pynchon's novel, like a lot of innovative contemporary fiction, aims to undermine this desire by showing how events rarely fit such simplistic linear chains. Joseph McElroy stresses a similar point late in *Women and Men* when a character reflects that although "the universe ran on cause-effect" it was distorted by passing "through some frame of curve he didn't really understand" (p. 979). In terms of plot, Wallace has significant affinities with these writers. As he observed in *The Broom of the System*, his aim is not linear simplification, but to show how one story has "to do with a context created by a larger narrative system of which this piece was a part" (p. 336). And rather than being isolated, *Infinite Jest's* three narratives are designed to suggestively interact, illustrating how individual action effects and is shaped by a larger community. But to understand how carefully Wallace has interwoven his narratives to show this, it is necessary to analyse the plot's synchronous development according to the novel's carefully structured chronology. It takes some time to map out how this works, but I think it is worthwhile partly because what actually happens in the novel may be unclear for many readers, but more importantly because the way events accumulate according to a tight temporal pattern tends to suggest interpretations itself.

Viewed in terms of its timeline, the narrative of *Infinite Jest* begins with an account of the Incandenza family in the 1960s, which then, in the last years of the century, branches into the complicating context of later stories. The chronologically earliest sections detail key incidents from James Incandenza's youth, and provide background information on his marriage to Avril Mondragon, which has been punctuated by his alcoholism and her infidelities. But as the millennium approaches, Wallace begins to use temporal contiguity to subtly pair characters like Hal and Gately. For example, according to an anecdote related by his unreliable brother, Orin, in spring 1997 Hal apparently eats some mold found in the basement of their Weston home. This incident, which is suggestively placed at the center of the novel's opening scene, is presumably intended to ominously foretell Hal's later involvement with DMZ, the powerful drug that "grows only on . . . mold" (p. 170). But it becomes apparent late in the book that this moment when Hal's later addiction is hinted at has been carefully timed to coincide with the failure of the "psychic emergency-brake" that has been controlling Gately's addiction (p. 906). In May 1997 he fails Sophomore Composition, and as he drops out of school for a year he loses all self-control and plunges into athletically crippling drug abuse. Because these events are related with nearly 900 pages between them, their coincidence can easily slip past the reader. But this subtle doubling can, in fact, be seen to be the characteristic method of the novel, and this becomes apparent as *Infinite Jest*'s chronology progresses.

Nearer the millennium, for example, such interconnections become more complex as Wallace begins to entwine the personal and the political. To do this, Wallace uses Orin's move to play professional football in 2001 as a focal point around which several important plot lines are paralleled. After Christmas, Gately watches Orin punting, and the contrast with his own wasted football talent launches him into a depression that climaxes with his imprisonment for assaulting two bouncers. In the same holiday season a crisis point also comes for Orin's girlfriend, Joelle van Dyne. On New Year's Eve, Joelle uses cocaine in front of Orin for the first time, and it is this habit that climaxes with her attempt to commit suicide eight years later. This personal unrest, however, is timed to coincide with political upheaval after Wallace's millennium. That same year, Rodney Tine is believed to have conceived of subsidized time, a sell-off that (according to Mario's fictionalized retelling of the story) was inspired by the sponsorship of a game that Orin played in.

When subsidized time is introduced in 2002, the map of North America has already been re-drawn with the creation of the Organization of North American Nations (ONAN). In this reconfigured map the United States has subsumed Mexico and Canada, with the leaders of these countries becoming secretaries of the larger entity. Individual borders have also shifted with a rough area north of a line from Syracuse, New York, to Ticonderoga, New York, and from Ticonderoga to Salem, Massachusetts, being forcibly ceded to Canada, and used as a dumping ground for the U.S. And again, this larger political action seems to be suggestively shadowed on the individual scale in the main narratives devoted to Gately and Hal.

While the United States is trying to exploit a three-way relationship with neighboring countries, Gately's partner-in-crime, Gene Fackelmann, is making a contemporaneous move to take advantage of a three-way transaction. After a misunderstanding over a bet between his employer, Whitey Sorkin, and his gambling client, Eighties Bill, Fackelmann attempts to profit massively from their momentary confusion by making off with both the apparent winnings and the supposed loss. But Fackelmann's bloody end (with which Wallace significantly decides to close *Infinite Jest*) is presum-

ably intended to prophesize the violence which reconfiguration will
bring.

Similarly, Hal's narrative seems designed to subtly echo the impact of reconfiguration. The year that subsidized time begins coincides with Hal's father developing a "delusion of silence" whenever
Hal speaks (p. 899), a move that is perhaps intended to reflect the
loss of Canadian and Mexican national voices.

The next few years are punctuated with significant events, as the
narrative gathers pace. In 2004, James Incandenza films *Infinite Jest*,
commits suicide on April 1, and is buried on April 5 or 6 in a small
town called St. Adalbert. In the same year Joelle's addiction becomes overwhelming, Gately starts taking Demerol, and the wheel-
chair-bound Québecois terrorists (the A.F.R.) begin a flurry of
killings. Two years later rumors of Incandenza's fatally-compelling
film apparently begin to circulate, but it is in 2008 that the crisis that
will ultimately entangle all three of the main narratives takes place.

While burgling a house in autumn 2008, Gately is unwittingly
responsible for the absurd death of Guillaume DuPlessis, the Québecois terrorist co-ordinator who has united and restrained many of
the anti-ONAN terrorist cells. As Gately does so, he also releases Incandenza's deadly *Infinite Jest* into the public domain when he
steals a copy from amongst DuPlessis's hidden collection of "upscale
arty-looking film cartridges" (p. 985n18). DuPlessis presumably has
a master copy of the film as a result of what a disguised James Incandenza referred to in 2001 as his "family's sordid liaison with the pan-
Canadian Resistance's notorious M. DuPlessis" (p. 30). It is proba-
ble, then, that this liaison has continued and that Avril, who was involved with the Québecois-Separatist Left in her youth (p. 64), has
supplied him with a copy of the cartridge. There seems little doubt
that the stolen cartridge is *Infinite Jest*, because, in an endnote to
this scene, Wallace refers to the "extremely unpleasant Québecois-
insurgents-and-cartridge-related" consequences of the theft (p.

985n16), and a little cross-referencing at this point show the cartridge's movements to be quite clear. It seems likely that when Gately, and his accomplice Trent Kite, divided up the spoils of the DuPlessis theft that Kite took the cartridges, as Wallace describes him just about drooling "at the potential discriminating-type-fence-value" of them (985n18). But who could Kite fence them to? The obvious suspect is Dr. Robert ("Sixties Bob") Monroe, "an inveterate collector and haggling trader of shit," who, Wallace tells the reader, sometimes "informally fenc[ed] stuff for Kite" (p. 927). This suspicion can be confirmed by working backward from the moment when the A.F.R. regain the film.

DuPlessis's *Infinite Jest* cartridge is "secured and verified" (p. 724) by the A.F.R. in the cartridge store that is run by two hapless Canadian terrorists, Lucien and Bertraund Antitoi, a location that the terrorists come to after tracing the film's path from "the young burglar" Kite to a "sartorially eccentric cranio-facial-pain-specialist" (p. 721). From the description given toward the end of the novel of Sixties Bob (p. 927), there is no doubt that he is the specialist referred to, and (as I discuss below) Wallace even describes the transaction between Sixties Bob and Bertraund Antitoi, allowing the movement of DuPlessis's copy of *Infinite Jest* to be plotted as:

Incandenzas → DuPlessis → Gately & Kite →
Sixties Bob → Antitoi Brothers → A.F.R.

But the film's circulation, as will become apparent, is a true circle, as the film that began in the Incandenza family, and was unleashed by Gately, ends back with them. In the meantime, however, DuPlessis's death in 2008 seems so contrived that few terrorists believe it is anything other than a deliberate ONAN killing, and the previously restrained cells are now free to act. At the same time, a remorseful Gately becomes convinced that a vengeful attorney, who has been waiting to settle a long-term grudge against him, will recognize his hand in this crime, so the penitent burglar decides to hide out in Ennet House. In the same autumn Gately stops taking drugs, while Hal begins getting high every day.

The consequences of this autumn begin to take shape in 2009 (Y.D.A.U.), which is the novel's most important year. On the fifth anniversary of James Incandenza's death, a copy of *Infinite Jest* is mailed to a Canadian medical attaché whose affair with Avril had been "especially torturing" to her husband (p. 957). Both the Québecois terrorists and the American agents (represented by Hugh Steeply) believe the film to have originated with Orin, but given how confused his responses are when he is tortured and questioned about the film at the end of the novel (p. 972), this is perhaps an error.

Toward the end of the year the chase for the film reaches its climax as the narratives begin to converge. In early November Joelle enters Ennet House, Hugh Steeply poses as "Helen" Steeply to interview Orin, the A.F.R. kill the Antitoi brothers and set up base in their misnamed store (Antitoi Entertainent), and Pemulis acquires the powerful drug DMZ. This last event, in particular, provides an especially neat demonstration of the way Wallace skillfully connects his narratives. Hal's first sight of the drug comes after Pemulis has purchased it on November 4. Pemulis has bought the drug from Tony Krause's acquaintances, the Antitoi brothers. Bertraund Antitoi traded a lava-lamp and a mirror to gain the drug (and DuPlessis's copy of *Infinite Jest*) from "a wrinkled long-haired person of advanced years in a paisley Nehru jacket" (p. 481). As becomes apparent nearer the end of the book, this is Sixties Bob, whose Nehru jacket and love of lava lamps are described along with his dealings with Gately (p. 927).

If Hal does ingest the DMZ, then this would explain why he remembers being in an emergency room in November 2009 (p. 16), and would give him the chance to meet Gately, potentially completing this neat circle. A further layer, though, is added by the fact that *Moment* magazine, for whom Steeply is posing as a journalist, has run an article on DMZ, so all three central narratives are carefully brought together around this incident.

Steeply is also present at the Eschaton brawl on November 8, watching from his "mint-green advertorial Ford sedan" (p. 327), and this scene is similarly arranged to subtly interweave the three narratives, with the wounded students ending in the same hospital as Gately after he is shot in the early morning of November 12. It is clear that Eschaton's Otis P. Lord is the figure in the bed adjacent to Gately, who seems to "have a box on its head" (p. 809), and in one of the novel's darker jokes, this is significant for reasons other than narrative intertwining. One of Gately's biggest problems with Alcoholics Anonymous has been his difficulty understanding the idea of a higher power, or God, and even as he lies in the hospital bed he begins to worry if God is really a cruel and vengeful figure, otherwise why would he have him "go through the sausage-grinder of getting straight just to lie here in total discomfort and have to say no to medically advised Substances" (p. 895)? His questions remain unanswered, but in the very next bed has been someone who not only shares a name with the Christian God (the "Lord"), but is hospitalized in the first place because they have been "more or less having to play God" (p. 328). Lord's wounds, of course, have resulted from his fallibility as Eschaton's god when he fails to control the consequences of a lapse in his omniscience, and his pathetic condition offers a sly correction to Gately's vision of a powerful deity.

Before Gately is hospitalized, however, the effects of the Eschaton debacle begin to filter through the tennis academy. Two days after the incident, Hal, Pemulis, Axford, and Kittenplan, are summoned to see Charles Tavis and an "urologist in an O.N.A.N.T.A. blazer" in an apparently official expulsion manoeuvre (p. 527). The phrasing here is, however, revealingly precise: it seems likely that this is not an actual tennis official, but an urologist impersonating one, an interpretation that is supported by the fact that a "blue blazer with an O.N.A.N.T.A. insignia" (p. 768) is hanging in Avril's office the next day. While the possibility that this is a staged test is evidently clear to Pemulis (who recognizes that a real ONAN tennis official would not be swayed by Avril's need to keep secret her sexual encounters with Wayne), it has a much bigger impact on Hal, who almost immediately vows to lead a substance-free life.

The next day, as his body struggles to overcome its chemical dependence, Hal comes surprisingly close to losing to Ortho Stice in a challenge match that coincides with Orin bedding the Québecois terrorist Mlle. Luria Perec, whose true identity is concealed under her disguise as a Swiss Hand model. And as the effects of Hal's withdrawal worsen, his face begins to resemble an unreliable mask, assuming "various expressions ranging from distended hilarity to scrunched grimace . . . that seemed unconnected to anything that was going on" (p. 966), and he loses control of the tone of his voice, though he is, at this point, still able to communicate.

Plotting the novel's chronological development like this may prove that, as James Incandenza's father observes in 1963, "synchronicity surrounds" (p. 493), but because of the way Wallace deliberately obscures the timeline toward the end of November 2009, it becomes difficult to establish what exactly happens in those last days and beyond. The final time we see Hal in Y.D.A.U. is immediately before the fundraising game that has been scheduled against Québecois opposition on Friday, November 20. In his last scene Hal is seen offering a pessimistic monologue on his own ontological stability, but what happens between this point and November of the next year is unresolved. We know from the novel's first section that sometime in November Y.D.A.U. he is in an emergency room, and we also know that at some point he digs up his father's head with Gately (whom he has yet to meet) while John Wayne watches. It is also clear that from February 2010 negotiations have been under way for Hal to join the University of Arizona, and although by November 2010 he is unable to take part in a simple conversation it is apparent that Hal can still function to a high-level of athletic excellence.

Wallace hints at (at least) three explanations that would resolve the mystery surrounding the missing year. Firstly, it could simply be marijuana withdrawal that is causing Hal's problems. This is certainly consistent with Pemulis's claim that Hal's decision to give up will result in him losing his mind, and dying inside (p. 1065n321). The second possibility is that Hal may have taken the ontologically disruptive DMZ. He suggests to the Arizona admissions panel at the start of the novel that they should attribute his problems to something he has eaten (p. 10), and the Weston mold-eating episode that Wallace follows this statement with suggests a parallel with the mold-based drug, as does his questioning of his own ontological status at the end of the book.

The logic of the novel, however, suggests that the third possibility is the most likely. Because on November 14 Marathe betrayed the A.F.R. by not revealing to them that Joelle was in residence at Enfield, it is possible that Hal has been a victim of the back-up plan of acquiring "members of the immediate family of the *auteur*" (p. 845) that the separatists turned to on November 19. This is the strongest explanation, partly because the A.F.R. have apparently hijacked the Québecois team bus, so the final time the reader sees Hal he is on the verge of being captured by them. It also seems to explain the strange references in the opening scene where Hal recalls the Canadian John Wayne "standing watch in a mask as Donald Gately and I dig up my father's head" (p. 17). He is presumably doing this because the film cartridge has apparently been buried with his father, and Wayne is standing watch because (it is hinted [p. 726]) he is working for the Canadian insurgents.

The question is then, if the film is there, do the A.F.R. make Hal, and perhaps Wayne, watch it? Common origins in an asbestos-mining town (p. 259, p. 1060n304) hint that Wayne's father is the disgraced Bernard Wayne, the only man to ever back out of one of the A.F.R.'s initiation rituals, so their motivation here would presumably be their punishment of the son for the sins of his father—a move that would be consistent with the novel's overall logic. And although Hal is clearly damaged, something much worse has evidently happened to Wayne that has left him unable to compete in the tennis competition Hal is playing in at the start. It is clear from the novel's climax that any stimulant has a heightened impact on Wayne's "cherry-red and virgin bloodstream" (p. 1073n332), so have the pair perhaps watched the film, with Hal ironically being saved by his prior exposure to addiction? Or has the rumored "anti-*samizdat* remedy cartridge" (p. 752) some role to play here?

Despite the evidence pointing to the third hypothesis, it is very difficult to confirm any of these explanations because Wallace has deliberately built a degree of ambiguity into the plot of his novel. Resolving the critical sections of the novel's interrelated lines of cause and effect hinges entirely on the missing year between November 2009 and November 2010. Because it is the chronologically most advanced section, the novel's opening is clearly critical to unravelling this mystery, but it offers suggestive hints, rather than solutions to the novel's puzzle. Even though the rest of the novel can be reconstructed in some detail, as Hal reflects elsewhere, there "is no map or You-Are-Here type directory on view" for the missing year (p. 798).

"THE UNFORTUNATE CASE OF ME" (p. 993n24)

While the first section of the novel is central to a chronological reading, it is also important because it introduces what turns out to be one of the obsessive themes of *Infinite Jest*: the search for an adequate understanding of the self. This melancholy exploration, which is largely (but not entirely) focused on Hal, partly explains why Wallace chose *Hamlet* as one of the templates for his novel. *Hamlet* begins with the question, "who's there?," and if Shakespeare's play answers this with an exemplary excavation of the consciousness of Renaissance man, then *Infinite Jest* attempts a millennial update, cataloging the twentieth century's endless efforts to understand itself. This anatomy of the contemporary self is instigated in the carefully orchestrated opening of the novel. Hal narrates:

I am seated in an office, surrounded by heads and bodies. My posture is consciously congruent to the shape of my hard chair. This is a cold room in University Administration, wood-walled, Remington-hung, double windowed against the November heat, insulated from Administrative sounds by the reception area outside, at which Uncle Charles, Mr. deLint and I were lately received.

I am in here.

Three faces have resolved into place above summer-weight sportcoats and half-Windsors across a polished pine conference table shiny with the spidered light of an Arizona noon. (p. 3)

Although the book begins with a confident assertion of identity, and geographical and chronological placement, the mock precision of this description of Hal's location only serves to highlight the elusiveness of his identity. It is clear that the cold room, sterilely cut-off from the external world, is meant to suggest a spatial metaphor for the hermetic husk of a self that "contains" this character who is unable to express his internal thoughts externally. Apart from the naming of the two E.T.A. officials who have accompanied Hal, his careful description is revealingly empty of human agency. Rich in data, but low on coherent identity, Hal projects his own marginal selfhood and presents the other five occupants as disconnected faces and heads, trying to resolve themselves into their larger identities. But as this section continues, it becomes clear that this struggle is more accurately his own, and given his failure to move beyond grunting and waggling to a more externally recognizable selfhood, the reader is forced to ask in what way can someone called Hal be said to be "in here": either inside the room, or, inside the body that is carefully manipulated by Charles and deLint. *Hamlet*'s question "who's there?" haunts this scene, and haunts the rest of the book.

The novel's opening, then, sets up a tension between an excess of information and unexplainable selfhood that is elaborated throughout the rest of the book. The exploration of this tension entails many different approaches and entangles most of the subsidiary themes of the book, but at the end of this scene, the answer offered to Shakespeare's question is that somebody unresponsive is there. And, appropriately for a novel that works in an encyclopedic mode, we are given an exhaustive account of how we could interpret this, as Hal explains: "There are, by the *O.E.D. VI*'s count, nineteen nonarchaic synonyms for *unresponsive*, of which nine are Latinate and four Saxonic" (p. 17). But turning to the dictionary's list of synonyms only goes to further confirm how the mystery of Hal's condition eludes classification. When Wallace wrote the novel, the latest edition of the *Oxford English Dictionary* was the second edition of 1989, which lists only two unrevealing synonyms for *unresponsive*: unable to reply, and irresponsive. While this "word-inflation" (p. 100) revealingly hints that Wallace's postmillennial world has become even richer in ways to be unresponsive than our own, it also serves to further highlight the lesson of the novel's fantastically precise opening: no matter how expansive your vocabulary, or how careful your description, a list of words is not enough to make a self.

It is significant, though, that if Hal is unable to tell us how he is "in here," he is surrounded by others who *are* trying. In this scene the Dean of Admissions relates the skeleton facts of Hal's life, and

Hal (again emptying an individual of uniqueness in favor of a generic type) acknowledges that he is "a personality-type I've come lately to appreciate, the type who delays need of any response from me by relating my side of the story for me, to me" (p. 3). Apart from the obvious fact that this personality-type relieves him of the need to interact with the external world, Hal perhaps also appreciates that this spares him the difficult task of self-definition. Hal notes that he has an "intricate history" (p. 11), and *Infinite Jest* suggests that much of this history has comprised of other's trying to define his character. This inability to define himself is subtly reinforced by the insertion into the middle of this section of one of Hal's childhood recollections that is, in fact, recalled by Orin, rather than Hal. And the status of this memory is further complicated by the fact that the second of the three times it is mentioned is alongside an anecdote that "may be a lie" (p. 1044n234a).

Moving forward in the book (and backwards in time) it becomes clearer how Hal's detailed history feeds into this first scene. In the admissions room at the University of Arizona, the interview panel initially suspect Hal of being "just a jock" (p. 10), but then learn that he is no one they can easily define. It is tempting to view this strangeness entirely as a result of some cataclysmic event that took place in the novel's missing year, but while that year and its missing events are obviously critical, the evidence of the novel as a whole prevents us from simply drawing that conclusion. In a monologue from three years earlier, for example, Hal has already explained how it is possible to be "neither quite a nerd nor quite a jock" but to "be no one." "It is easier than you think," he says (p. 175).

But although Hal recognizes himself as a selfless "no one," he is not immune to the multitude of explanations of selfhood that surround him. At the academy, in particular, Wallace suggests that his sense of self has partly been molded by a book that is described as "inescapable-at-E.T.A." (pp. 281–82): Edwin Abbott's *Flatland* (1884).

Flatland is a quasi-mathematical exploration of a world that exists solely in two dimensions (length and breadth), and so the reasons why it would be taught on three courses at a tennis academy whose founder adopted a coldly mathematical take on tennis are fairly obvious. The players are presumably encouraged to meditate on the significance of line, depth, and sphere, in a more abstract way than when bounded by the lines of the court. But the influence of Abbott's description of the two-dimensional self seems to have extended beyond tennis philosophy for Hal, and perhaps Orin, too. Hal has understood himself "for years as basically vertical," and as his lack of depth begins to depress him at the end of the book, it is notable that his response is simply to shift within the limits of two dimensions and become "horizontal" (p. 902). In addition, along with Orin, he apparently views staff at E.T.A. as if they were inhabitants of Abbott's two-dimensional Flatland: he tries, for example, "to get to the side of" Aubrey deLint, to see whether he "has a true z coordinate or is just a cutout or projection" (p. 460), while Orin sees Tavis as "less like a person than like a sort of cross-section of a person" (p. 517).

Perhaps more importantly, though, as *Infinite Jest* is a novel that explores the different ways "fathers impact sons" (p. 32), Wallace places Hal's problems with self-definition in a longer perspective that details the legacy of his father. According to the evidence of the filmography Wallace includes, James Incandenza apparently also felt that he was surrounded by a multitude of explanations of the self. And although Joelle describes his filmic quest as a search for "freedom from one's own head" (p. 742), an escape from the self that perhaps shares something with his son's sense that he is no one, he seems paradoxically to have sought that freedom by attempting an encyclopedic survey of efforts to understand the self in his films.

Incandenza's survey ranges from the fanatically literal exploration of the self in *"Every Inch of Disney Leith,"* a film made up of "minituarized, endoscopic, and microinvasive cameras" traversing "the entire exterior and interior of one of Incandenza's technical crew" (p. 989n24), through *"The Man Who Began to Suspect He Was Made of Glass,"* where a man undergoing psychotherapy believes himself to be "brittle, hollow, and transparent to others" (Ibid.), to *"Immanent Domain"* (p. 987n24), which stages a contest between neuroscience and psychoanalysis. But if these attempts to understand the self suggest that Hal's definitional problems simply stem from his father, it is notable that the chronology of *Infinite Jest* encourages us to look further back, and factor James's father into the equation as well.

It is surely significant that the novel is arranged so that the chronologically earliest section features James's father offering what will turn out to be a seminal definition of what a self is. The son has been taken down to the communal garage to begin the teaching that will make him a top collegiate tennis player, but in a move that seems to have serious implications for the later tennis academy, James's father sets about his tuition not with any outline of tennis basics, but with a mini-lecture on the self:

Son, you're ten, and this is hard news for somebody ten, even if you're almost five-eleven, a possible pituitary freak. Son, you're a body, son. That quick little scientific-prodigy's mind she's so proud of and won't quit twittering about: son it's just neural spasms, those thoughts in your mind are just the sound of you're head revving, and head is still just body, Jim. Commit this to memory. Head is body. Jim, brace yourself against my shoulders here for this hard news, at ten: you're a machine (p. 159).

For all the novel's wider references to phrenology (p. 521), or "Developmental Psych." (p. 738), it is the definition established in this

monologue that sets the boundaries for the struggle that later characters in general, and Hal in particular, have with explanations of the
self. The elder Incandenza collapses the Cartesian distinction between mind and body, and offers an account of consciousness that
leaves little space for traditional conceptions of selfhood. This re-
ductionist strategy is recognizably materialist.

At its most basic, materialism is the school of thought that holds
that all phenomena, no matter how complex, are explicable in terms
of material processes that operate at a more fundamental level (in
the sciences, this is typically at the atomic, or sub-atomic level). But
considered specifically within the philosophy of mind, materialism
is a monistic thesis that does away with appeals to "soul" or "spirit"
in its insistence that mind is simply an emergent phenomenon of
the biological matter of the brain. In this scene Wallace subtly
stresses the importance of the materialist definition of the self that
the senior Incandenza offers by his choice of narrative technique
(the entire section is narrated externally, allowing no insight into
some privileged inner realm of the self), but the centrality of this
thesis to the novel is also stressed by the symmetry of the novel's
temporal pattern. Wallace has set his work up so that this earliest
section is recalled fifty years later (in the chronologically most advanced section of the novel) when Hal is still defending himself
against the specific definition of his grandfather when he explains to
the panel at Arizona that "I'm not a machine" (p. 12). In chronological terms the book literally begins and ends with materialism.

The implications of Incandenza's belief that his son is a machine
that his tuition can perfect eventually entwine most of the major
themes of the book (tennis, addiction, consumerism), but it is worth
briefly noting that this is one of the ways in which Wallace attempts
"to do something real American" ("Salon Interview," p. 4). Viewed
historically, the search for the machine-like perfection of the self
could be seen as a characteristic American obsession, traceable back

to the inception of the Republic when spokesmen like the physician Benjamin Rush spoke of the need to convert men into perfectible "Republican machines" (p. 92) who would make up the new country. Similarly, when Hector St. John Crévecœur announced the arrival of that new species, the American, in his *Letters From an American Farmer* (1782), he observed that the settlers "were machines fashioned by every circumstance" of the new environment around them (p. 73). Wallace's account of the mechanical "perfectibility of man" (p. 968), then, suggests *Infinite Jest*'s continuity with early American literature, but the immediate context of the materialist explanations of the self in the novel draw on a more recent body of writing.

The 1990s had been designated the "Decade of the Brain" by the senior George Bush, an act of naming that was designed to draw the public's attention to the benefits that could result from neuroscientific research. And although earlier American writers, such as Don DeLillo and Joseph McElroy, had already begun to explore the imaginative possibilities of the neuroscientific map of the mind, the elevated profile Bush's designation conferred brought with it an increase in the number of popularized accounts of how the material of the brain (its bewildering network of neurons) could produce something as ethereal as consciousness. While it seems likely that Wallace was already well-informed about neuroscience, it is perhaps not entirely coincidental that as *Infinite Jest* was published in the middle of the 1990s it shares that decade's fascination with science's materialist accounts of the mind.

In fact, given that materialist explanations of the mind seem to be everywhere in Wallace's post-millennial world, it may be that one of his aims is to trace the impact of this sponsored psychology. In 2009, even late-night documentaries attribute schizophrenia to the topography of positrons emitted by the "dysfunctional brain" (p. 48), while government agents discuss "neurotransmitters" (p. 471). It is notable, however, that despite this ubiquity, materialist references consistently cluster around the players at E.T.A. in particular.

The whole program at the academy, particularly under Gerhardt Schtitt (whom James Incandenza "wooed fiercely" to persuade him to work at the academy [p. 79]) is geared toward "self-forgetting" (p. 635), and in practice this seems to involve encouraging the young players to forget traditional ideas of the self and see themselves in materialist terms. In what the reader is presumably meant to recognize is a hereditary chain from James Incandenza's father the players consistently adopt the machine language of some branches of neuroscience in their self-descriptions. Troeltsch schools younger players about how the accretive weight of repetitive training makes movements "sink and soak into the hardware, the C.P.S. . . . wiring them into the motherboard" (p. 117–18); Wallace describes "the player's different CPU's humming through Decision Trees" (p. 629); and Hal limits his work according to the talents he is "hardwired" for (p. 852). This perhaps explains why *Flatland*, with its depthless selves, is so common at E.T.A., but it also connects to the critique of television Wallace outlines in his essays. The pro-circuit that all the players are aiming for is memorably known as "The Show" in the novel. And, like the shallow TV-selves Wallace describes in his essay, these successful players become "pictures in shiny magazines" (p. 388), two-dimensional magnets for envy and admiration. The intensive schooling in loss of self at E.T.A., then, is preparation for the TV-like show where the young players will get "made into statues" (p. 661).

Significantly, it is the academy's top players in particular who have managed to become the most machine-like. John Wayne is a "grim machine" (p. 438), who has the prized ability of shutting "the whole neural net down" (p. 96). He shares this talent with the highly-rated Ortho Stice, and Wallace makes his mechanized selfhood explicit in his darkly-humorous observation that "if you could open Stice's head you'd see a wheel inside another wheel, gears and cogs being widgeted into place" (p. 635). For Hal, too, this has increasingly become the case.

Although, in 2008, Hal was only "a respectable but by no means to-write-home-about" player (p. 259), in the year leading up to November 2009 he has made a competitive leap that now puts him second in the academy. In line with the novel's logic this has involved the collapse of the distinction between his mind and body, though Hal noticeably reverses the movement when he remarks, "for the last year his arm's been an extension of his mind" (p. 689). In an apparent culmination of his grandfather's programme, Hal's emergence as a top player is at the peak of his mechanical selfhood.

But while his narrowed-down identity seems to have been inherited from the sports psychology of his forefathers, it is part of a complicated bequest that is reinforced by their legacy of addiction. To appreciate this, though, it is necessary to search for the rare moments when Wallace reveals the young players' interiors. Again, the temporal arrangement of the novel is revealing. If the start and end of the chronology of *Infinite Jest* are designed to stress the novel's exploration of the limits of materialist accounts of the self, then it is important to note that the timescale also suggests a break in the strict exteriority of such accounts. The important date here, both inside and outside the novel, is November 8.

The celebrations at E.T.A. on November 8 are introduced with the Latin *"GAUDEAMUS IGITUR"* (p. 321), a phrase from a medieval student song that translates as: "let us therefore rejoice." But while the redrawing of the map of North America may offer little cause for festivity in the Incandenza household, there are other reasons to celebrate on November 8. On that date in 1895, for example, the German physics professor Willhelm Conrad Roentgen was working into the night in his laboratory in Würzburg. While preparing an experiment on cathode rays, Roentgen accidentally discovered X-rays when he passed a current through a partially-evacuated glass tube shrouded in cardboard and made a chemically-treated paper glow on the other side of the room.

Roentgen's discovery allowed scientists to literally see inside a human being without dissection for the first time in history. But while this obviously had medical applications, its impact extended far beyond the scientific community. Popular magazines reacted with a mix of hysteria, and commercial greed to Roentgen's pictures of human interiors, as the primitive horror the images prompted was gradually replaced by the consumer consolation of the chance to buy a picture of your own soul.

Infinite Jest evokes this historical context by making two apparently incidental references to X-rays in sections that take place on November 8: on the day that Joelle arrives at Ennet House (which Wallace later confirms as "11/8" [p. 1025n134]), Wallace tells the reader of Bertraund Antitoi's "fraudulent but seductive X-ray spectacles" (p. 481); and the Interdepenence Day Eschaton game depends upon Otis P. Lord calculating the impact of every "thousand Roentgens of straight X and Gamma" unleashed (p. 330). But these ostensibly casual references are significant because Wallace has organized the chronology of his novel so that a number of key revelatory events in *Infinite Jest* cluster around November 8. The anniversary of the date when Roentgen saw inside himself is the date in the novel when, at E.T.A., the masks start to come off and the hidden interiors are revealed.

This is most explicit in the Eschaton episode. Although the game's combatants have been carefully schooled at E.T.A. toward loss of self and the goal of machine-like functionality, the events of the afternoon of the 8th November reveal the selves they have been taught to hide: the previously repressed rage and frustration that the younger students have for each other end in a massive fight; Pemulis's "blue-collar Irish" heritage comes out (p. 334), as does the long-term resentment he has for the Penn family; while for James Struck the loss of control and revealed interior are more literal, as he collapses and wets himself. But while the consequences of these self-revelations lead to larger disclosures later in the novel, the most significant interior that is revealed on November 8 undoubtedly belongs to Hal.

Like the others, Hal has some fairly straightforward moments of self-knowledge that afternoon. He suspects that he may be "a secret snob about collar-color issues and Pemulis" (p. 335), and he is unable to conceal the contempt he has for "Sleepy T.P." Peterson's inability to define the word *"equivocationary"* (p. 337). But the scene is ordered so that Hal's self is also more dramatically exposed. The Eschaton section ends with Wallace describing "a brief moment that Hal will later regard as completely and uncomfortably bizarre," as Hal "feels at his own face to see whether he is wincing" (p. 342). This stark recognition of self-alienation is carefully placed here because, although Hal's divorce from himself has been apparent since the opening scene, it is on November 8 that Hal reveals his previously hidden marijuana addiction.

But what is the connection between Hal's alienation from himself and the revelation that his need for marijuana has increased to the point where it overwhelms his love of secrecy? Timothy Melley's observations on the logic of addiction are illuminating here. In his study, *Empire of Conspiracy* (2000), Melley argues that a perception of addiction develops as a result of a pervasive sense of insufficient free will. Behind these anxieties, he argues, lie a number of assumptions about the self:

First, one must believe individuals *ought to be* rational, motivated agents in full control of themselves. This assumption in turn entails a strict metaphysics of inside and outside; that is, the self must be a clearly bounded entity, with an *interior* core of unique beliefs, memories, and desires easily distinguished from the *external* influences and controls that are presumed to be the sources of addiction. (pp. 162–63)

That Hal's loss of control over his addiction, then, is carefully timed to coincide with his loss of control over the expressions that should be most personal to him is presumably intended as a literal manifestation of the disintegration of the last of his inner core of self. The inner gaze on November 8 reveals only emptiness, and with this recognition comes the inevitability of defeat in his efforts to limit his addiction, and estrangement from the self follows. But while Hal's alcoholic father and grandfather have bequeathed their addiction to him, as outlined above, they have also passed down a sporting philosophy that depends upon the extinction of the idea of an "inner" self. And here emerges the significance of the coincidence of Hal's competitive explosion and the year of his addiction. Both have drawn on the same erasure of self. Shortly after Hal has reflected on his past year's growth, in a passage that is both heavily shadowed by the ghost of his father (his family name "Himself" recurs, while his initials, J.O.I., are played on) and clearly designed to echo the novel's fourth sentence, Hal describes this empty self:

Hal himself hasn't had a bona fide intensity-of-interior-life-type emotion since he was tiny; he finds terms like *joie* and *value* to be like so many variables in rarified equations, and he can manipulate them well enough to satisfy everyone but himself that *he's in there*, inside his own hull, as a human being — but in fact he's far more robotic than John Wayne. . . . inside Hal there's pretty much nothing at all, he knows. (p. 694, last italics mine)

Although at times *Infinite Jest* may suggest the outlines of a conventional *bildungsroman*, tracing the development of a sensitive prodigy through an institutional upbringing, the movement of the novel is actually away from fully-realized selfhood. It charts the progressive erasure of identity by the pressures of family and academy. And it is notable that while Joyce's *A Portrait of the Artist*, which is perhaps the ultimate template of a sophisticated twentieth-century development narrative, begins in the third person and ends in the first, *Infinite Jest* reverses this pattern. Beginning with a confident "I," the narrative proper ends with "he." But including the endnotes, the last of which is "Talwin-NX—®Sanofi Winthrop U.S." (p. 1079n388), the movement traced by the novel is from the personal, to the impersonal, to the corporation. Receding circles of alienation from the self.

"NO TROY" (p. 990n24)

While this first section, then, acts as an overture to the complex performance of the rest of the book, the second section seems to represent a deliberate falling away from its thematic and dramatic intensity. Having lured the reader in with the compelling strangeness of Hal's situation and the intellectual suggestiveness of his thought, the shift to the drama of waiting may seem flat by comparison. But this section is subtler than it may at first appear. It is, for example, quite carefully constructed to contrast Erdedy's movement from the start, where he "sat and thought" (p. 17), to the end, where he stands, addicted, "without a thought in his head (p. 27), and it also extends some of the themes from the opening section. In particular, Hal's revelation of the limits of encyclopedic knowledge in his account of "unresponsive" is replayed in the helplessness of Erdedy. As an educated graduate Erdedy is easily spotted later by Gene Martinez as one of the worst sort of addicts, the kind of person who will "identify their whole sel[f] with their head" (p. 272). And, as the second section shows, this assessment of Erdedy is accurate. Knowledge has allowed him to manipulate a woman into thinking that he is addicted to methamphetamine hydrochloride (he can convince her because he has "researched the subject carefully" [p. 23]), and only needs the marijuana she can supply to stem his more rapacious desires. But knowledge is not power for Erdedy, and his inability to control his addiction through his skill as a researcher is ironically exposed when nearly two hundred pages later we discover him in Ennet House.

This theme is reinforced later in the novel when the "data cleric" (p. 69), Kate Gompert, is similarly found recovering in the halfway house, but the second section is also important because it introduces the reader to one of the fundamental obsessions of the novel: perspective. In the carefully ordered opening, Wallace reveals three different scales of action:

Erdedy . . . sat and thought. He was in the living room. When he started waiting one window was full of yellow light and cast a shadow of light across the floor and he was still sitting waiting as that shadow began to fade and was intersected by a brightening shadow from a different wall's window. There was an insect on one of the steel shelves that held his audio equipment. The insect kept going in and out of one of the holes on the girder's that the shelves fit into. (p. 17)

Beginning with the human scale, Wallace then contrasts it with the perspective of a larger natural cycle in which the human is dwarfed, the path of the sun. Shifting scales again, Wallace then moves to the microlevel of the insect, a scale in which the otherwise helpless Erdedy has the power of life and death. These three scales are carefully interwoven, and although this is obviously in part a humorous exposure of how addiction has diminished the scale on which Erdedy can impact the world, it also has a larger relevance for the rest of the book. While Erdedy manages no more than a vague intuition of the relation between these perspectives (he feels "similar to the insect inside the girder . . . but was not sure just how he was similar" [p. 19]), the overall movement of Wallace's novel is constantly to encourage the reader to locate the local in larger perspectives.

As I have tried to show earlier in this chapter, one of the ways Wallace does this is by placing his characters in a longer evolutionary perspective, showing how the apparently individual is just one link in an extended hereditary chain. But *Infinite Jest* also demonstrates how the individual action takes place within more complex systems, beyond their comprehension. An incident involving Gately provides a good example here. On November 8, Gately is driving to an upscale store in Inman Square, while chewing over his personal concerns about Pat Montesian's running of Ennet House. As he drives:

> one piece of the debris Gately's raised and set spinning behind him, a thick flattened M.F cup, caught by a sudden gust as it falls, twirling, is caught at some aerodyne's angle and blown spinning all the way to the storefront of one "Antitoi Entertainent" on the street's east side, and hits, its waxed bottom making a clunk, hits the glass pane in the locked front shop door with a sound for all the world like the rap of a knuckle. (p. 480)

Although Gately is acting according to his own personal agenda, his actions intersect with the other two main narratives (the film *Infinite Jest* is inside the store, and from this store the A.F.R. try to infiltrate the Incandenza family) and create a number of unsuspected patterns in the novel. Because Gately stole the film that is now in the Antitoi store, his passing impact makes a small narrative circle, reconnecting his passing sober self with the film that he stole as an addict. A dark symmetry is also established. The apparent knock that Gately's passing creates brings Lucien Antitoi to the door of his store, to check for visitors. But this mistaken announcement of a visitor prefigures the imminent visit of the A.F.R. who are about to murder the Antitoi brothers.

This is typical of the way *Infinite Jest* works, and there are many other incidents in the novel that illustrate this kind of interconnection. The circular movement of Incandenza's film, and the passage of the DMZ, for example, are paradigmatic examples of the novel's "circular routine" (p. 53). While each of the characters act individually in their localized environment, their individual actions have multiple connections to lives and narratives beyond their comprehension. And their apparently random interactions tend to form large-scale patterns (and particularly circular patterns) in the novel. This movement from lower-level action to higher-level pattern is characteristic of emergent networks. As Steven Johnson, in his study *Emergence* (2001), summarizes, an emergent system involves "multiple agents dynamically interacting in multiple ways, following local rules and oblivious to higher-level instructions" with these interactions resulting "in some kind of discernible macrobehavior" (p. 19). In many ways this seems an apt description of *Infinite Jest*'s circular ordering, and it is not coincidental that this arrangement resembles the interconnected "systems inside systems" of natural ecologies (p. 67).

This similarity is humorously introduced when Marathe mispronounces "recycling" as "recircling" (p. 643), but it is of more serious importance to the novel because the largest perspective that the novel places the individual in is that of the Earth's ecosystem. In fairly obvious ways Wallace's work dramatizes the disastrous impact of man's excesses on the natural world: the stockpiling of toxic waste in the Concavity has apparently produced teratogenic clouds, carnivorous flora, and feral hamsters. And these ensuing mutations cast an ironic light on the novel's second section: if Erdedy towers over the insect in this scene, the rumored mile-high toddlers that have developed in the Concavity (p. 670) obviously reverse this hierarchy dramatically.

Ecological change, however, is not confined to the darkly humorous exaggerations of Wallace's future, but is, in fact, shadowed by the novel's real geography. The town of Enfield, where most of the novel takes place, has (like the cities of the Concavity) disappeared off the American map to satisfy the resource-drain of larger urban centers. Along with three other towns (Dana, Greenwich, and Prescott), Enfield was flooded in August 1939 when the Swift river was dammed to create the 40 square miles of the Quabbin reservoir and provide the Greater Boston area with water. Wallace was presumably aware that Enfield was "one of the stranger little facts that make up the idea that is metro Boston" (p. 240) because Amherst has special collections of Quabbin Towns Materials, and while this subtly reinforces the novel's ecological theme, it also emphasizes some of *Infinite Jest*'s more melancholy preoccupations. In preparing to flood the area all the lost town's dead had to be excavated and reburied, a fact that seems darkly appropriate for a novel that is partly about the returning dead.

While the novel, then, sets its action within literally different scales, it also dramatizes them on different ontological levels. Ontological complication is, according to Brian McHale in *Postmodernist Fiction* (1987), a characteristic postmodern strategy. In his neat formulation of the transition from modernism to postmodernism, McHale argues that the movement can be understood as a shift from a modernist poetics preoccupied with epistemological concerns (problems of knowing) to a postmodern practice dominated by ontological concerns (questions of being). So, for McHale, a work like Robert Coover's *The Universal Baseball Association* (1968) is an exemplary text of postmodernism, inasmuch as Coover's work sets up an ontological contest between a "real" world and a fictional one, that results in the "real" world of the text being swamped by its apparently subordinate fiction.

On first inspection, *Infinite Jest* may seem to be working on similar principles, as the novel consistently teases us with hints of ontological complexities. The effects of the drug DMZ are "almost ontological" (p. 170), Hal suspects he is "broadcast" rather than real (p. 966), some sections of the novel are excerpts from fictional books rather than dramatized components of the narrative (such as pp. 491–503), while some of the works cataloged in James Incandenza's filmography are temptingly similar to episodes recounted in the book (compare pp. 27–31 and the description of the film "*It Was a Great Marvel That He Was in the Father Without Knowing Him*" [p. 993n24]). But, in line with Wallace's desire to break with postmodern recursion, much of the ontological layering in *Infinite Jest* resembles modernist, rather than postmodernist, practice. *Ulysses* again offers a revealing example here.

While *Ulysses* ostensibly traces in great naturalistic detail the paths of two Dubliners round the city, their journeys are famous for the larger patterns they suggest. Through an elaborate framework of carefully arranged parallels, Joyce makes their passage suggestive not just of *Hamlet*, but also of the trials of *Odysseus*. But while *Ulysses* may seem to pre-empt much postmodern fiction, it maintains what McHale calls a "unified ontological plane" (p. 234): although Stephen Dedalus may echo Telemachus, the reader does not suspect that he will become Telemachus *rather* than Stephen Dedalus. And if *Infinite Jest* does not depend upon the kind of extreme ontological uncertainty of McHale's postmodernism, Wallace does seem to have attempted to "create a mythology" (p. 515) within the work that recalls Joyce's mythic frameworks.

Given that *Infinite Jest* is so unusually rich in references to Greek mythology, this seems the obvious place to look for mythic parallels. At different points in the book Agamemnon, Achilles, Cerberus, Helen, and Troy, are all mentioned. But the attempt to locate *any* mythic pattern in the novel initially seems unpromising. When the young Don Gately wishfully imagines himself as the loyal and fierce "Sir Osis" (p. 449), the pun on the cirrhosis that is killing his mother darkly undermines the possibility that his character might be seen in a larger heroic light. It seems at this stage that the novel is deliberately distancing itself from the mythic past. But ironically, it is when Gately is reluctantly forced to adopt a traditionally heroic role that we are given the first hints that he might also be meant to represent a "Greek mythic personality" (p. 529).

Having been compelled by Lenz's viciousness to defend the tenants of Ennet House from burly retribution-seeking Canadians, Gately takes a gunshot wound to the shoulder. After subduing his assailants, he lies down next to Joelle who, uncharacteristically for an Ennet House section, is here referred to as "Madame Psychosis" (p. 618). Her radio name is, of course, temptingly close to "metempsychosis" (a word of Greek origin, that means the migration of the soul from one body to another) and as she tries to comfort him the stars in the night sky above begin to "shine right through people's heads" (p. 617). This may seem an incidental description doing little more than demonstrating the effects of shock and pain on Gately's consciousness, but there is little in this long book that does not serve some larger purpose. And references elsewhere in the novel that detail the merging of the stars and characters' heads make this scene seem to hold particular clues to Gately's mythic metempsychosis.

The key scene to cross-reference here is from the long night at the end of April that Rémy Marathe and Hugh Steeply spend above Tucson. As dawn approaches, Marathe describes the night sky: "The legs of the constellation of Perseus were amputated by the earth's horizon. Perseus, he wore the hat of a jongleur or pantalone. Hercules' head, this head was square." (p. 507). As the reader has been informed more than two hundred pages earlier, Gately is also distinguished by "a massive square head" (p. 277), and the parallels between Heracles and Gately are compelling.

On the most simplistic level, the parallels involve both characters committing unintended murders. Heracles murders his wife and children while temporarily insane from a spell cast upon him by Hera, and Gately commits an accidental murder during a burglary he has been driven to by his addiction to oral narcotics. In recompense for these offenses, both undergo a series of trials. Heracles, famously, is given twelve tasks to perform before he can go to Thebes to marry, while AA also denies Gately relationships and imposes an identical number of duties upon him: the twelve steps of its rehabilitation program. Despite both praying to a higher power during their trials, however, they must still contend with the continued bitterness of powerful figures from their pasts. Heracles continues to be a target for Hera's interference, while a remorseless North Shore Assistant District Attorney pursues Gately.

On a more important level, though, this mythic pattern significantly supports some of the critical information about the missing year that Hal alludes to in the novel's opening section. For example, in the only reference to this year, Hal remembers Wayne watching as "Donald Gately and I dig up my father's head" (p. 17), and it is significant that this tessellates with the novel's mythic logic, as the last task of Heracles requires him to travel down to the underworld to bring Cerberus up to the surface, a feat he accomplishes by seizing the dogs' heads. But this mythic pattern also directs the reader to consider the larger significance of other characters. For a start, it is notable that as Marathe sees a constellation in the sky that resembles Gately, he also describes a truncated Perseus that recalls his own legless condition, and (although less extended) the parallels are again suggestive. Perseus was the son of Zeus and Danaë, and is most notable for slaying the Gorgon Medusa with the help of Athena, the goddess of prudent warfare. But while the multiple attachments Marathe maintains to America and Quebec may not be prudent, the effect of watching the entertainment *Infinite Jest* is, as

Steeply suggests (p. 529), only an inversion of the effect of looking on the Medusa. Marathe, then, with his doctrine of exemplary self-control and denial, may on one level be intended as a sort of antidote to the entertainment. A slayer of its fatal gaze.

As Marathe looks at the brightening sky, he notes that these constellations make it seem "as if giants were looking over his shoulder" (p. 508), and the mythic patterns that lie behind both him and Gately suggest that this is a fair description of the narrative's multiple levels. But the hidden patterns of *Infinite Jest* are not solely drawn from Greek mythology, and an even subtler overlay seems to surround the problematic blind young tennis player Dymphna.

Dymphna appears to present a problem in the text for a number of reasons. Firstly, the conflicting reports of his age seem a glaring example of a breakdown in Wallace's authorial control. Early in the novel, for example, Hal reports Dymphna's age as "sixteen" (p. 17), but on two later occasions he is described as only "nine" (pp. 518, 567). Secondly, it is unclear whether he is actually blind or not. At the start there seems no doubt that he is, as he plays with sonic balls designed for blind players. But later, the reader is told that he has "several eyes in various stages of evolutionary development," and is only legally blind (p. 518). Thirdly, his roots are ambiguous. At different points his origins are given as Illinois, Iowa, and Ticonderoga via Illinois. Perhaps Pemulis comes closest to the truth when he ironically places him as a native of "Nowheresburg" (p. 567). All this uncertainty is compounded by the fact that he never actually appears in person anywhere in the novel, which may make it seem odd that Wallace included him in the novel at all, let alone in the crucial opening section.

But in actual fact, Dymphna seems to be one of the most important characters to the overall plan of the novel. Although the name is revealing absent from the *O.E.D.*'s exhaustive survey, Dymphna (sometimes Dympna) is a Catholic saint, thought to date from the seventh century. Her mother died, and her father conceived an incestuous obsession for her, which resulted in her flight and death, and because of this history she is invoked in cases of epilepsy, family unhappiness, loss of parents, mental disorders, and by psychiatrists. With the notable exception of addiction, it is surely important that this list encircles most of the problems that dog Hal, with psychiatrists (who would try to explain his self) especially near the top of his list. It may be that Dymphna, who "appears to always have floated by magic to the necessary spot" (p. 568), is intended to arrive as some sort of spiritual antidote for Hal.

This raises the possibility that *Infinite Jest* may basically be a religious book. Although this might seem unlikely, it is clear that, on one level, the novel is about belief. Whether Wallace is documenting Marathe's bitter reflection that "the presence of Americans could always make him feel vaguely ashamed after saying things he believed" (p. 318), or Mario's discomfort that "real stuff can only get mentioned if everybody rolls their eyes" (p. 592), the spiritual hollowness of a life without belief seems to be one of the most persistent themes. And in a short introductory essay to a special issue of the *Review of Contemporary Fiction* entitled "The Future of Fiction" that was published in the same year as *Infinite Jest*, Wallace revealingly commented:

To me, religion is incredibly fascinating as a general abstract object of thought—it might be the most interesting thing there is. But when it gets to the point of trying to communicate specific or persuasive stuff about religion, I find I always get frustrated and bored. I think this is because the stuff that's truly interesting about religion is inarticulable. (pp. 7–8)

In line with this, the apparent religious subtext of the novel is not explicitly articulated but, like the mythic resonances surrounding Gately, it provides an enriching texture to the otherwise desolate narrative of Hal. Despite his paralyzing addiction and empty self, the novel intimates that belief may provide, as the last words hint, a "way out" (p. 981).

"INSUBSTANTIAL COUNTRY" (p. 992n24)

In placing so much emphasis earlier in this chapter on how *Infinite Jest's* plot unfolds according to a precise chronology, I hoped not only to help newcomers to the novel begin to map out what actually happens in the book, but also to respond to those critics who have found the work careless and chaotic. But the precision of the novel's temporal arrangement is also significant for reasons other than the synchronous layout of Wallace's complex plot outlined above. The dates on the calendar itself are carefully arranged to suggest a subtle layer of historical meaning to the narrative, with significant dates recurring.

As always, this works on several levels. On a relatively superficial level, for example, it is notable that the traditionally unlucky date of Friday 13th coincides with Gately's hospitalization. It is just five minutes after midnight on November 12, when the Canadian duo come to Ennet House in search of Lenz (p. 610), and despite his protests, Gately is taken to the Trauma Wing of St. Elizabeth's Hospital later on the twelfth. Time passes indistinctly for Gately in the hospital, but one of the few times when Wallace does clearly identify the date is when he notes that it is "Gately's first full night" in the hospital (p. 810), which presumably carries the reader into (or at least to the brink of) Friday 13th. Significantly, this is also the first time that the "shadow of somebody in a hat" (Ibid.) is described, apparently signifying the revenge hungry attorney waiting outside the room. Unlucky, the reader infers, for Gately.

In a further layer, it is notable that this fight with the Canadians was instigated on November 11 — Remembrance Day in the U.K. —

when Lenz "remembered" his drug addiction, and Gately experiences a "surge of Remember-Whenning" (p. 610) as he enters the conflict. Such chronological parallels turn out to form a consistent pattern in the novel, although the significance of the dates often depends upon more sophisticated connotations than in this instance. For example, the first section of the novel to be headed with a precise date is the third section, which takes place on April 1, 2003, and the implications of this date are multiple. Most straightforwardly, April 1 is April Fool's Day, which suggests that James Incandenza's disguise as a professional conversationalist is a joke (however you want to interpret this), but given the terrible events that occur on it (this desperate attempt to communicate with his son, as well as his later suicide) an echo of Eliot's observation in *The Waste Land*, that "April is the cruelest month," is perhaps also intended. Crucially, though, the historical origins of April Fool's Day suggest a more important interpretation. In France, April 1 had previously marked the start of the new year until the sixteenth-century when Charles IX introduced the Gregorian calendar. News of this spread slowly, however, and outside the urban centers many continued to celebrate the new year on the old date, and were designated "fools" by those with better sources of information. In 2003, in Wallace's novel, the calendar has recently been changed again, and the repetition of significant events in James Incandenza's life on April 1 is perhaps designed to mark his resistance to this switch.

Later in the novel, April 1 is also the date that the medical attaché receives the copy of *Infinite Jest* that kills him, and at the end of that month Marathe and Steeply meet above Tucson to discuss his death. Once more, the selection of date is deliberate. Marathe and Steeply talk through the night of April 30 and into the morning of May 1. This, of course, is May Day, whose origins lie in a festive holy day for the ancient Celts and Saxons who celebrated the first spring planting, and Wallace seems to have drawn on James Frazer's massive anthropological study, *The Golden Bough* (1890–1922) to elaborate upon its significance here. According to Frazer, the Celts marked this celebration by lighting bonfires on hills. In some Scottish rituals these sacred fires acted as a community's moral barometer and if any of the fire starters "had been guilty of murder, adultery, theft, or other atrocious crime[s], it was imagined either that the fire would not kindle, or that it would be devoid of its usual virtue" (p. 717). Frazer's list of offenses noticeably summarizes the three major crimes of the novel—the murder of DuPlessis, Avril's adulteries, and Gately's theft of the film—and, intriguingly, on the floor of the desert below Steeply and Marathe's outcrop, they see the flickers of a "celebratory fire" (p. 422), but the flames are "burning in a seeming ring instead of a sphere," as Marathe expects (p. 423).

Saxonic fire festivals also seem to be alluded to. As Marathe and Steeply begin their meeting the previous night, so Saxons began their celebrations on April 30, marking the end of winter and the return of the sun by igniting wooden wheels. But, as Frazer observes, "the eve of May Day is the notorious Walpurgis Night, when the witches are everywhere speeding unseen through the air on their hellish errands" (p. 721). Wallace alludes to this context by specifically comparing his setting to Goethe's *Walpurgisnacht* in *Faust* (p. 994n38), but the scene has its own, quite precise, internal significance. The May Day fires that celebrated the end of April were partly designed to ward off witches, and it is surely significant that a web of references in the novel identify Avril (which is, of course, French for April) as a witch. Her personal study in Headmaster's House has a picture of the *Wizard of Oz*'s "West Witch on the door" (p. 191—itself mysterious, as there are "no interior doors between rooms" in the building [p. 189]), and on the critical revelation date, November 8, she wears a "steeple-crowned witch's hat" (p. 380).

The Golden Bough also seems to illuminate a strange occurrence in Y.D.A.U. At the start of that year, selected toothbrushes have been mysteriously coated with "betel-nut extract" (p. 1077n352) for reasons that no one at the academy can decipher. According to Frazer, however, the setting out of betel nuts is an important ritual in some East Indian cultures to mark the arrival of the new year. It is appropriate, then, that the betel nut extract appears at E.T.A. in January and February, but Frazer also observes that this Javan ritual is "at the same time a festival of the dead" (p. 377), with the nuts being set out as an invitation for the family dead to return. And this seems to tessellate with the dating of events later in the year.

Most of the rest of the action from Y.D.A.U. takes place in the autumn, and it is not accidental that a number of festivals of the dead fall in this period: November 2 marks the Day of the Dead in post-conquest Mexico, for example, while Halloween (which is more important to the novel) falls on the last day of October. The origin of Halloween seems to lie with the ancient Celtic tribes who used to celebrate the new year on November 1. The previous night was the eve of *Samhain* when, as the old year died, the Celts believed the veil between the spirit world and their own grew thin, and the dead were permitted to return. The Celts lit bonfires and wore masks to protect themselves from evil spirits, but as the Christian church gained power it sought to outlaw such druidic festivals. The persistence of belief in the returning dead, however, meant that this was very difficult to do, so (as Frazer recounts) the church instead attempted to absorb the celebration in 835 AD by placing the Christian celebration of All Saints' on the date of Celtic New Year's Day.

In part, this contributes to the novel's historical account of political manipulation of the calendar, but the importance of these dates to the narrative clearly goes beyond such overarching patterning, because (as with the May Day fires below Marathe and Steeply) on some level the characters seem to be aware of this hidden significance. Lenz, for example, echoes ancient rituals when he contemplates a human sacrifice "near Halloween" (p. 546), masks are referred to throughout the novel with revealing frequency, and perhaps most importantly, in the autumn burglary of the DuPlessis home that unwittingly results in so much death, Gately and Kite protect themselves by wearing Halloween masks (p. 56).

Despite its setting in the near future, the deeper chronological pattern of *Infinite Jest* frames the novel's action in a vast temporal perspective reaching back hundreds of years. Played out against this dark background, *Infinite Jest* is clearly a book with "wide-ranging and deeply hidden themes having to do with death and time" (p. 644).

At the end of chapter one I suggested that, despite its differences, *Infinite Jest* possessed significant similarities to the earlier encyclopedic narratives that are strategically poised on the brink of apocalypse. And the death obsessed calendar of the novel contributes to other hints that the reader may be about to witness "one day's apocalypse" (p. 339). The narratives clearly move toward an apocalyptic collision, while 2010 is "the very last year of O.N.A.N.ite Subsidized Time" (p. 1022n114), and the hidden calendar of the novel suggests that, as in "all quality eschatologies" (p. 1043n234), a feast of the dead is imminent.

3

The Novel's Reception

"THE UNIVERSE LASHES OUT" (p. 989n24)

"Limitations of space and patience," a character reflects in *Girl with Curious Hair*, are "a constant and defining limitation these quick and distracting days" (p. 357), and Wallace's decision to write a book that neither made concessions to reduced attention spans nor was easily assimilated to traditional fictional templates inevitably received some mixed reviews. Many reviewers offered superlatives, others were critical, while some, like Lisa Schwarzbaum, who reviewed the novel for *Entertainment Weekly*, showed a level of refreshing honesty. "Skimming isn't possible," Schwarzbaum announced, "reading the last page first reveals nothing." The size of the book, she learns, makes it tricky to read in bed, so her review raises "a limp white flag" of surrender.

But if the very size of the novel defeated many readers, Wallace's publishers recognized its mass as a potential selling point quite early on. In a somewhat unpleasant article for the *New York Times Magazine* (the author apparently goes through Wallace's medicine cabinet), Frank Bruni quotes Little, Brown's head of marketing, who revealed that they planned to play the novel's size as indicative of its importance: "the size lent a certain weight to the book, that there was a certain undeniability about it." And even before the book was released, a market for it had been created by a skillfully organized planning campaign. Bruni reports that:

the company compiled a list of 4,000 booksellers, industry insiders and media types and sent out a staggered series of six postcards that cryptically heralded the release of an at-first-unspecified book that gives "infinite pleasure" with "infinite style." And when blurbs to that effect became available from other authors and critics, Little, Brown put them on postcards and dispatched another series of three.

This initial interest was strengthened by a round of reviews that included influential writers like Sven Birkerts, Tom LeClair, and Jay McInerney. Birkerts' review, "The Alchemist's Retort," was published just two years after he had critiqued contemporary novelistic ambition and announced that, "no one thinks any longer about writing the Great American Novel" (p. 207) in his post-mortem of reading, *The Gutenberg Elegies* (1994). But in the intervening period, he had evidently reconsidered this position, and his very positive review praises *Infinite Jest*'s innovations:

Wallace is, clearly, bent on taking the next step in fiction. He is carrying on the Pynchonian celebration of the renegade spirit . . . tailoring that richly comic idiom for its new-millennial uses. To say that the novel does not obey traditional norms is to miss the point. Wallace's narrative structure should be seen instead as a response to an altered cultural sensibility. The book mimes, in its movements as well as in its dense loads of referential data, the distributed systems that are the new paradigm in communication.

His review also makes a case for the novel's emergence from one of Wallace's earlier essays, and details *Infinite Jest*'s affinities with Gaddis and Pynchon, but one of its omissions is particularly revealing. While most reviewers, understandably, made minor errors in their summaries of Wallace's complex novel, perhaps the most surprising and consistently-made mistake was failing to recognize that Gately and Hal's narratives eventually merge, as revealed in the novel's opening section. Birkerts, for example, argues that the multiple plot lines "do not come to apocalyptic or even transfiguring intersection," when, it is, of course, the implied apocalyptic intersection of the narratives that is the novel's climactic (though undramatized) event. He was, however, far from alone in this omission.

Michiko Kakutani, who reviewed the novel for the *New York Times*, for example, also insisted that a reader who harbored even "the vaguest expectations of narrative connections" (p. B2) would be left reeling from the novel's randomness. Kakutani also had predictable reservations about the novel that centered on the size of the work and Wallace's supposed self-indulgence. Although she praises Wallace as "one of the big talents of his generation, a writer of virtuosic talents who can seemingly do anything," her praise is mingled with apparent impatience, as she claims that the book "often seems like an excuse for Mr. Wallace to simply show off his remarkable skills as a writer and empty the contents of his restless mind" (Ibid.).

In his review for the avant-garde journal, the *American Book Review*, Tom LeClair praises the novel's "profound cross-class study of parental abandonment and familial dysfunction" (p. 16) and although he makes the odd small error (mistaking Ken Erdedy for Hal in the novel's second section) his attention to nuance makes the review one of the most insightful *Infinite Jest* received. But because it reads more like a précis for his important essay on the novel (see chapter four), I will omit it from lengthy examination here. A similar note was struck, however, in the review published in the *Review of Contemporary Fiction*. But while LeClair stressed Wallace's Pynchonian heritage, this review by Gaddis-scholar Steven Moore neatly traced the novel's encyclopedic ancestry back through the decades to Gaddis's *The Recognitions*. Moore's assessment of the novel tends toward the superlative, praising an "amazing command of late-twentieth-century English" that extends even beyond Pynchon and Gaddis (p. 141), and he sums the work up as "both a tragicomic epic and a profound study of the postmodern condition" (p. 142).

Jay McInerney's review for the *New York Times Book Review* evaluated the novel in rather colder terms. Finding the book "alternately tedious and effulgent" (p. 8). McInerney's appraisal is typically couched as censored commendation, often prefacing praise with reproval: while there are, he writes, "many uninteresting pages in this novel, there are not many uninteresting sentences." Like nearly all the other reviewers McInerney invoked a comparison with *Gravity's Rainbow*, but he also registered important differences: "despite the *Gravity's Rainbow*-plus length and 'haute science' flourishes, Mr. Wallace plays it . . . almost realistically—and seems to want to convince us of the authenticity of his vision by sheer weight of accumulated detail" (Ibid.). And it is the weight of this accumulation of detail, alluded to in both the first and last sentences of the review, that seems to form the crux of his essay.

Many other reviewers went for the safety of a balanced judgement, like Steve Brzezinski's assessment in the *Antioch Review*, which reports that the book "brims with erudition, wit, and stylistic brilliance, yet its sheer length enervates" (p. 491). But one of the most cutting notices came from another novelist, Dale Peck. According to his review, "Well, duh," which appeared in the *London Review of Books*, Peck was particularly unimpressed with the novel. Peck evidently hated *Infinite Jest*, and although his criticisms are occasionally humorous ("I would, in fact, go so far as to say that *Infinite Jest* is one of the very few novels for which the phrase 'not worth the paper it's written on' has real meaning in at least an ecological sense" [p. 14]) his errors and misreadings are grave, and of various kinds. While it is hopefully clear from the last chapter that Peck's assertion that the novel is "uncontrolled" does not stand up to close analysis, his claim that Marathe and Steeply have "a 700-page conversation" is just plain wrong. They have a 61-page conversation. As already noted, Peck also fails to identify the work's chronology, while he more seriously misinterprets what he identifies as the novel's thesis when he argues that Wallace fails to recognize that "the really insidious thing about the U.S. entertainment fetish is not that it's forced on us, but that we choose to give over so much of our lives to this crap" (Ibid.). It is surely clear to most readers of *Infinite Jest*, however, that Wallace *is* showing a culture *choosing* to indulge their love of entertainment. As LeClair noted in his review, Wallace is showing a generation of happy victims who seek a "pleasure that deforms and destroys." The coercion in the novel arises not from people being forced to view something they have no desire to see, but from the frenzied race to possess the film. More positively, though, Peck does offer quite a good summary of Wallace's prose style, describing the:

important aesthetic at work in Wallace's prose . . . There is a faux sloppiness about his prose that enables him to discuss with varying degrees of fluency all sorts of subjects—Wittgenstein, Descartes, calculus, physics, 12-step programmes, tennis—without resorting to academese . . . whenever his hold on his material is a little shaky, he can hide behind the stutter of an ellipsis or a burst of expletives . . . it can actually allow Wallace to tell his readers things he doesn't know (p. 15).

It is perhaps useful, however, to put Peck's negative account in context, because his recent reviews make it easy to dismiss his criticisms. His acidic review of Rick Moody's *The Black Veil* (2002) in the *New Republic*, dismissed most of the twentieth-century's better writers (from Joyce, through Nabokov, to DeLillo) and effectively undermined Peck's claims to aesthetic standards. The questions his reviews ultimately raise are perhaps personal, rather than literary critical: why does he continue to put himself through the ordeal of reviewing novels that he evidently finds so distasteful?

But while most of the work's early critics found something to praise in the novel, the most disappointed reader of the book was undoubtedly Katherine A. Gompert. Having played on the same junior tennis circuit as Wallace, Gompert was presumably less than happy to discover that she shared a name (and not a name, you would have thought, that might have occurred coincidentally) with a suicidal drug addict in the novel who admitted she was a *"shitty lay"* (p. 782). Shortly after the paperback release of the book, Gompert's case was filed, and Judge James Ware summarized the circumstances as he issued an order denying an attempt by the defense to have the case thrown out in May 1998:

Plaintiff was a successful junior and college tennis player and then competed on the professional tour . . . she enjoys a good reputation and has often spoken to younger tennis players regarding the importance of leading a drug-free lifestyle. Plaintiffs allege that David Wallace, the author, purposely defamed her to satisfy his own feelings of hatred and malice towards her. Mr. Wallace apparently participated in the competitive junior tennis world in which plaintiff was well known.

Although unsuccessful, her legal action provided an unpleasant contrast to the praise that had followed the publication of *Infinite Jest*, but since then the novel has received rather lengthier evaluation.

· **4**

The Novel's Performance

"AS OF YORE" (p. 991n24)

At the end of William Gaddis's encyclopedic masterpiece, *The Recognitions*, the life work of a dedicated composer is described as "still spoken of, when it is noted, with high regard, though seldom played" (p. 956). In an irony that Gaddis seems to have appreciated, for nearly thirty years this was largely the fate of his long novel, with "read" substituted for "played." Perhaps because literary postmodernism, as it was canonized in the 1960s, drew on a backdrop of the splintering of knowledge where no metalanguage was possible, works like *The Recognitions* that invoked the encyclopedic dream of total knowledge seemed anomalous and were rarely discussed by critics concerned with new writing. *The Recognitions* was thus dismissively reviewed, and was (on those occasions when it was mentioned) treated as a belated modernist monster.

And for many later encyclopedic American novels the fate of *The Recognitions* was paradigmatic. Although the exceptions, like *Gravity's Rainbow*, are notable, learned and innovative novels such as McElroy's *Women and Men*, Vollmann's *You Bright and Risen*

Angels, Gaddis's *JR* and *A Frolic of His Own,* and Gass's *The Tunnel,* have each been noted for their ominous scale and difficulty, and then casually omitted from larger discussions of contemporary writing. According to the terms of Franzen's argument, they have been categorized as "status" works, and (except for a few specialists) even academic readers have rarely approached them. Thus stigmatized, the possibility that they might offer rich rewards if approached as "contract" works has been overlooked in talk of their "difficulty" and "erudition." Although Jack Gibbs in *JR* complains that "the whole God damned problem's the decline from status to contract" (p. 393), the problem for these books has often been that their standing as status works has declined so slowly.

In light of this, the number of readers that *Infinite Jest* has found is heartening. Perhaps partly through clever marketing, or perhaps because the internet has allowed communities of readers with similar tastes to find each other and spread the word, Wallace's novel seems to have escaped the initial small audiences that *The Recognitions* and earlier encyclopedic narratives suffered, and has gained a large readership despite the much reported drift away from print media. In terms of academic attention, too, *Infinite Jest* has established itself faster than its literary ancestors. While ten years passed before the first academic essay devoted to *The Recognitions* appeared, Wallace's novel received intelligent analysis within a year of its publication in Tom LeClair's essay, "The Prodigious Fiction of Richard Powers, William Vollmann, and David Foster Wallace."

LeClair's essay was influential not only because it drew the attention of critics to sophisticated novels by these three writers, but also because it outlined a context in which they could be examined. Like many reviewers, LeClair approaches these writers from the perspective of Pynchon's legacy, but his particular angle involves considering the younger writers' expertise with information systems alongside Pynchon's scientific knowledge. In the short section that focuses ex-

clusively on Wallace, LeClair discusses several of the novel's references to science alongside its fascination with "prodigies," and also
explores how the novel can be read as a response to contemporary
fiction. Given how closely it followed the publication of *Infinite Jest*,
it understandably includes an occasional error (the observation that
"Gately's father became an obsessive watcher of M*A*S*H" [p. 32],
should properly refer to Steeply's father [p. 639]) but this overview
should be required reading for students of the novel.

Later essays devoted to Wallace's writing seem to confirm the centrality of *Infinite Jest* to his oeuvre. Although Wallace had been highly
thought of as a writer before the publication of his big novel (his work
had shared a special issue of the *Review of Contemporary Fiction* with
William Vollmann and Susan Daitch in 1993), and despite the subse-
quent publication of *Brief Interviews With Hideous Men* in 1999,
Wallace's current reputation depends overwhelmingly on *Infinite Jest*.
Perhaps because it is both more serious than his other work, and has
greater scope, it has so far received the lengthiest elucidation, in articles that betray an illuminating variety of approach.

A particularly good introductory essay is Frank Louis Cioffi's
"'An Anguish Become Thing,'" because Cioffi concentrates at
some length on the experience of reading the book. Cioffi's essay
examines *Infinite Jest* as an example of what he calls the "disturbing
text," and although he makes a slight error by doubting whether
Joelle has been disfigured (p. 166)—there may be some uncertainty
because the major source of information is the unreliable Molly
Notkin, but given that Orin is referred to as "dodger of flung acid
extraordinaire" by the narrator early in the book (p. 223) it seems
reasonable to assume that her account of Joelle's disfigurement (p.
795) is accurate—his overall reading is valuable because of his attention to the novel's verbal landscape.

Another useful early essay is Timothy Jacobs' "American Touchstone," which offers an intelligent discussion of Wallace's essay on

television as a way into a detailed examination of the surprising over-laps between Wallace's millennial aesthetic and the Victorian poet Gerard Manley Hopkins' radicalism. Arguing that "both stress the importance of flux within constraints, and discipline fused with cre-ative variety" (p. 229), Jacobs supports his reading with detailed ref-erence to the novel and Wallace's interviews.

It is revealing that Catherine Nichols, in an essay published in the same year, comes independently to a somewhat similar conclu-sion as Jacobs by following a quite different route. Approaching the novel from the perspective of the Bakhtinian carnivalesque, Nichols also contends that the novel's aesthetic lies in a balance between innovation and tradition, when she argues that Wallace "turns the carnivalesque against itself to reveal a literary vision that foregrounds the line between transgression for its own sake and the use of art for redemptive purposes" (p. 3).

N. Katherine Hayles's 1999 essay, "The Illusion of Autonomy and the Fact of Recursivity," situates the novel amid a larger argu-ment over the relation of the self to freedom, natural ecologies, and virtual environments. The essay is not for the easily daunted, but its attempt to demonstrate that *Infinite Jest* "shows that the idea of an autonomous liberal subject can be a recipe for disaster in a world densely interconnected with interlocking complex systems" (p. 696) is perceptive.

Infinite Jest has also begun to receive analysis in longer works that survey the wider field of contemporary fiction. Although in some studies, like Robert Rebein's *Hicks, Tribes, and Dirty Realists* (2001), it is invoked somewhat casually as a convenient example of a big book with which others can be contrasted, in others it is considered more critically. The brief discussion in Joseph Tabbi's *Cognitive Fic-tions* (2002), for example, provides an interesting response to earlier criticism as it breaks with the prevailing trend of considering *Infinite Jest* as an extension of Pynchon's work.

Frederick Karl's survey, *American Fictions: 1980–2000* (2001) includes a lengthier discussion of Wallace's novel, which Karl sees as an opportunity to extend his earlier analysis of post-war "Mega-Novels." Karl's entertaining overview is written in a far looser vein than its comprehensive precursor, *American Fictions 1940/1980* (1983), but still offers valuable insights, such as rightly identifying "annular" as one of the novel's key words, and generally mapping its literary context (p. 474). Karl does, however, tend to over-stress the chaotic aspects of the novel, arguing that the disorder of Wallace's world "is of such magnitude that any effort to harness [it], by the author or by an outside force, is futile" (p. 473). I hope this guide provides a corrective to such claims.

Perhaps a more significant register of Wallace's achievement, though, has been the response of other writers. Novelists like Don DeLillo, Richard Powers, Jonathan Franzen, Lawrence Norfolk, Jeffrey Eugenides, and Zadie Smith have each expressed their admiration for his work, with Smith admitting that "Wallace is proving to be the kind of writer I was sort of hoping didn't exist—a visionary, a craftsman, a comedian and as serious as it is possible to be without writing a religious text" (p. 9).

Perhaps more marginally, Dave Eggers's memoir-novel, *A Heartbreaking Work of Staggering Genius* (2000), is connected with Wallace's novel inasmuch as it explores some similar themes to *Infinite Jest*, and features an enthusiastic blurb from Wallace. Eggers clearly shares Wallace's interest in critiquing what *Infinite Jest* calls postmodernism's "absolution via irony" (p. 385), and it also seems to carry a subtle allusion to Wallace's novel. A little over halfway through, Eggers expresses his fears that Toph will "grow up to kill kittens by putting them in garbage bags and swinging them against brick walls" (p. 256), a nasty habit that parallels Randy Lenz's in *Infinite Jest*. Given the other overlaps, this aside may be intended as a form of what *Infinite Jest* calls "the sort of deep-insider's . . . tribute no audience could be expected to notice" (p. 65).

Further Reading and Discussion Questions

"WAVE BYE-BYE TO THE BUREAUCRAT" (p. 990n24)

There are a vast number of websites devoted to Wallace but they are of varying quality. And perhaps because many sites sprang up as a response to the hype surrounding *Infinite Jest*'s publication, in the following years many have become outdated. There is, however, a lively discussion list that readers can subscribe to by visiting:

<http://waste.org/mail/?list = wallace-l>

Two sites that have a range of valuable links to on-line Wallace materials, are also worth a visit:

The Howling Fantods:

<http://www.geocities.com/Athens/Acropolis/8175/dfw.htm>

Reviews, Articles, and Miscellany:

<http://www.smallbytes.net/~bobkat/jesterlist.html>

Other valuable resources include:

Wallace's *Review of Contemporary Fiction* interview with Larry McCaffery:

<http://www.centerforbookculture.org/interviews/
interview_wallace.html>

Audio files of Wallace in conversation with John O'Brien and Richard Powers:
<www.lannan.org/_authors/wallace/index.htm>
Tim Ware's concordance to the novel:
<http://members.aol.com/russillosm/ijndx.html>

DISCUSSION AND PAPER IDEAS

In terms of further study, *Infinite Jest* is almost (as is publicity boasted) infinitely rewarding. However, because of the way it uses repetition within its large scale, the reader is apt to develop the kind of paranoia about hidden meanings that Don Gately adopts as a staffer at Ennet House, asking suspicious residents: "Is that supposed to mean something? What's that supposed to mean?" (p. 1044n245). But there are a number of patterns that repay further study.

1: Hal shares his name with a computer in Stanley Kubrick's film, *2001*. *Infinite Jest*, itself, is about a film and a filmmaker, and Wallace has written about David Lynch. Taking the convergence of these three points as a starting point, explore the relationship between the novel and film.
2: Grammar and languages provide a revealing thread throughout the novel: the narrative is set in motion when DuPlessis dies because he does not speak English, and Gately does not speak French; the monolingual Lucien Antitoi dies sounding a call "in all the world's well-known tongues" (p. 489); and the grammatical precision of Avril is a constant presence at the academy. Investigate the significance of this alongside Wallace's essay, "Tense Present: Democracy, English and the Wars over Usage" that appeared in *Harper's* (April 2001).
3: Wallace makes the novel's *Hamlet* parallels explicit in his choice of title, and the family pattern of usurpation and ethereal fathers, but *Infinite Jest* also includes a web of more complex allusions to Shakespeare's play. Trace these, and explore the possible significance of other Shakespeare plays (particularly *Henry IV* series) to the book.

4: In some ways the novel is about both transcription and plagiarism. Hal, for example, transcribes Pemulis's words for the Eschaton manual, and Wallace likes to draw attention to the novel as a mediated work with the insertion of phrases like "Pemulis doesn't actually literally say 'breath and bread'" (p. 1025n130). Plagiarism is a theme that begins in the first two scenes—Hal is accused of plagiarism by the admissions panel, and Erdedy's former partner was an "appropriation artist" (p. 24)—and periodically resurfaces. Examine the significance of this alongside the pious forgers of *Finnegans Wake* and *The Recognitions*.

5: As essays like "Greatly Exaggerated" show, Wallace is clearly aware of developments in poststructuralist criticism over the last few decades. Can the stretches of the novel that detail an author returning from the grave to explain how his "radical realism" (p. 836) has been misunderstood, be read as an oblique commentary on Roland Barthes's "The Death of the Author"?

6: Wallace's account of the self seems to draw on two sources in particular: Gilbert Ryle's *The Concept of Mind* (1949), which Hal's grandfather seems to have read, and A. R. Luria's *The Man with a Shattered World* (1972), which may have helped inspire Hal's condition (as it seems to have inspired DeLillo's *Great Jones Street* [1973], a novel that *Infinite Jest* in many ways resembles). Explore *Infinite Jest*'s intertextual dialogue with these two works.

7: There is some quite subtle interplay with initials in the novel—with both James O. Incandenza and Avril M. Incandenza containing ironic jokes in French. Is there a contradiction here between Wallace's quest for fuller characterization, and this reduction of his characters to a linguistic existence?

8: Compare *Infinite Jest*'s use of its size and range to other contemporary works in the encyclopedic field like Powers's *The Gold Bug Variations*, Evan Dara's *The Lost Scrapbook*, and Lawrence Norfolk's *Lemprière's Dictionary*.

9: This study outlines the way Hal falls away from selfhood. Examine this loss of identity in terms of similar passages in earlier works, such as the disintegration of Slothrop in *Gravity's Rainbow*, or the movement in *The Recognitions* which traces the central character's transformation from Wyatt, through an identity neutral "he," and the Swiss Stephan, and finally to Stephen.

Appendix

THE CHRONOLOGY OF

INFINITE JEST

"THE AMERICAN CENTURY AS SEEN THROUGH A BRICK"
(p. 989n24)

This skeleton chronology is designed to help the reader navigate the temporal disruptions of Wallace's complex fictional map. However, as what the novel calls "an unpleasant-fact specialist" (p. 22), I feel obliged to point out that there are a number of chronological problems in the novel, such as those surrounding the month of Mario's birth (first given as May [p. 54], then November [p. 312]), and the date Stice freezes to a window (discovered by Hal early on November 18 [p. 865], but not removed until November 20 [p. 909], though he takes part in a conditioning run in between these times [p. 899]). Such problems may derive from the fact that a number of characters in the novel frequently lie, or they may be errors on the part of the publisher, or they may result from Wallace's desire to make his chronology as suggestive as possible, but where there is doubt, I have gone with the date that seems to be most consistent with the overall plan of the novel.

1933: James Incandenza's father suffers career-ending knee injury (p. 167).

1950: James Incandenza born (given that he is 54 in Dove Bar [p. 64]).

1953: Avril born (given that she is 56 in Y.D.A.U. [p. 766]).

1960: James Incandenza Senior takes his son down to the garage to begin his tennis training (pp. 157–69).

1961: When Avril is 8 years old, her mother dies (p. 900) of an "infarction" (p. 953).

Charles Tavis born (given that an oblique reference suggests that he is 48 in Y.D.A.U. [p. 314]).

1962: James Incandenza's father retires "from a sad third career as the Man from Glad" (p. 313/date given p. 1022n114): he had "served for two years" (p. 492).

1963: *Winter*: 13 years old, James Incandenza becomes "interested in the possibilities of annulation" (p. 503).

1981: Don Gately born (given that he is 27 in Y.D.P.A.H. [p.55] and 28 in Y.D.A.U. [p. 277]).

1983: Orin born (given that he is 9 years older than Hal [p. 314], and 26 in Y.D.A.U. [p. 598], and two years younger than Gately [p. 916]).

1985: 4-year-old Gately lives in a little beach house in Beverly with his mother and "Herman" the breathing ceiling (p. 809).

1989: Pemulis's father comes "over on a boat from Louth in Lenster" (p. 683).

1990: When Gately is 9, his mother is first diagnosed with cirrhosis (p. 449); Gately also smokes "his first duBois at age nine" (p. 903).

1991: Tavis arrives at E.T.A. the "spring" before Mario's birth and "after the horrible snafu with the video-scoreboard at Toronto's Skydrome" (p. 312).

James Incandenza's mother dies of emphysema "shortly before Mario's surprise birth" (p. 953).

Mario Incandenza born (given that he is 18 in Y.D.A.U. [p. 54])

1992: Cult of the Next Train develops (p. 1058n304)?

June: Hal born (given that he is eleven in Y.T.M.P. [p. 27]).

October: Michael Pemulis born (given that his 17th birthday is in Y.D.A.U. [p. 152], and 13th in Y.P.W-C. [p. 218]).

John Wayne born (given that he is 17 in Y.D.A.U. [p. 1069n324]).

1994: Gately does "his first Quaalude at age thirteen" (p. 903); until he is 15 he is a "devotee of Quaaludes and Hefehreffer-brand beer" (p. 904)

1997: The M.I.T. language riots take place after the Militant Grammarians of Massachusetts convention (p. 987n24).

March or Early April: Hal apparently eats some mold from his family's Weston basement (p. 10).

May: Gately fails "Sophomore Comp." and withdraws from school for a year to preserve his junior season (p. 906).

1998: James Incandenza first spots John Wayne "at age 6" while working on *Homo Duplex* (p. 260)

Late October (p. 906): During Gately's last season playing football he discovers his mother has had a cirrhotic hemorrhage; Gately smoked his "first gasper" that day (Ibid.).

After leaving school, Gately works for the bookmaker Whitey Sorkin (p. 911).

1999: From the age of seven, Hal resides at E.T.A. (p. 4).

From the age of 18–23, Gately and Gene Fakelmann serve "as like Whitey Sorkin's operative in the field" (p. 912).

2001: Age 20, for "about a year" Gately lives in a loft with an addicted nursing student in Malden (p. 843).

Orin "got out of competitive tennis when Hal was nine and Mario nearly eleven" (p. 283).

Orin's first game against Syracuse was "in its last season of representing an American University" (p. 294).

"dark legend" has it that "Subsidized Time was conceived on the back of a chintzy Chinese-zodiac paper placemat, by R. Tine" in a "famous Vienna, Virginia Szechuan steakhouse" (p. 411).

"*after Xmas*" (p. 915): Gately watches a "B.U. punter" (Orin) while forging drivers licenses and begins to cry.

"*two days later*" (p. 916): Gately is arrested for assaulting two bouncers.

New Year's Eve: "the last P.M. Before Subsidization, was the first time Orin saw Joelle ingest very small amounts of cocaine" (p. 296).

[2002] Year of the Whopper: "for several months before he did his State assault-bit" Gately is involved with Pamela Hoffman-Jeep (p. 924).

While Gately is on bail for three months (p. 917), Fackelmann exploits Sorkin and Eighties Bill.

March: "three months after" Gately watched Orin, he went to Billerica Minimum (p. 916).

"ecologically distorted and possibly mutagenic territory" forced on Canada (p. 1056n304).

The Experialist Migration (p. 93).

Ennet House founded (p. 137).

James Incandenza begins to have "this delusion of silence" when Hal speaks (p. 899).

[2003] **Year of the Tucks Medicated Pad:** Joelle makes her "first appearance in a James O. Incandenza project . . . *Low-Temperature Civics*" (p. 707).

1 April: James Incandenza poses as professional conversationalist (p. 27).

Orin alleges "that when he took the Mom's car in the morning he sometimes observed the smeared prints of nude human feet on the inside of the windshield" (p. 899).

August: this would be the date that Gately was released from Billerica, and took up breaking and entering with Kite (p. 918).

24 November (Thanksgiving—although it is on 27th in 2003): Joelle's mother kills herself with "kitchen garbage disposal" (p. 788), and Joelle is disfigured (p. 795).

[2004] **Year of the Trial-Size Dove Bar:** James Incandenza "quit drinking in January . . . It was something Joelle was real specific about" (p. 249).

James Incandenza shot *Infinite Jest* "at the start" of this year— "less than ninety days later" he died (p. 230).

March: James Incandenza "went in for another detox" (p. 249).

1 April, after lunch: James Incandenza, at the age of 54 (p. 64), "stopped living" (p. 249).

1 April, before 16:30: Hal finds his dead father (p. 250).

"*5 or 6 April*" (p. 910): James Incandenza buried in St. Adalbert, a small town "fewer than five clicks west of the Great Concavity" (p. 910).

"almost twelve," Hal has nightmares (p. 63).

Joelle "has been in a cage since Y.T.S.D.B." (p. 227).

Age 23, Gately starts taking Demerol (p. 891).

Autumn: flurry of A.F.R. killings (p. 1057n304).

[2005] **Year of the Perdue Wonderchicken:** Hal last saw Orin (given that in Y.D.A.U. he hasn't seen him for "four years" (p. 1015n110).

The Madame Psychosis show begins (p. 591).

Age 24, Gately gets pleuritic laryngitis "sleeping on the cold beach up in Gloucester" (p. 833)

[2006] **Year of the Whisper-Quiet Maytag Dishmaster:** Rumors of the "ultimate cartridge-as-ecstatic-death" begin to circulate (p. 233).

Gately loses his driving license "for getting pinched on a DUI in Peabody on a license that had already been suspended for a previous DUI in Lowell" (p. 462).

[2007] **Year of the Yushityu 2007 Mimetic-Resolution-Cartridge-View-Motherboard-Easy-To-Install-Upgrade For Infernatron/InterLace TP Systems For Home, Office, Or Mobile (*sic*):** Ken Erdedy goes through an "outpatient treatment program" (p. 20).

"Hal tore all the soft left-ankle tissue he then owned at fifteen . . . at Atlanta's Easter Bowl" (p. 457).

April: "Tennis and the Feral Prodigy" film gets an honourable mention in Interlace's young filmmakers contest (p. 172).

6? November: Hal, Pemulis, Struck, Troeltsch "and sometimes B.Boone have made a little ritual of nipping out to the little hidden clearing behind West House's parking lot's dumpsters and sharing an obscene cigar-sized duBois before the I.-Day-Eve expedition" (p. 1018n110).

[2008] **Year of Dairy Products from the American Heartland:** *Spring:* John Wayne recruited by Aubrey deLint and Gerhardt Schtitt (p. 259).

"John Wayne's Québecois and Canadian citizenships . . . revoked" (p. 262).

"roughly the second month after his arrival" Wayne becomes sexually involved with Avril (p. 957).

Summer: *Infinite Jest* comes to the attention of Unspecified Services (given that in early November Y.D.A.U. this happened two summers past [p. 548]).

Autumn: Don Gately accidentally kills Guillaume DuPlessis (p. 59).

10 September: Possibly the last day that Gately ingests narcotics (given that he has been "completely substance-free for 421 days" [p. 274]).

November: From at least this point, Hal spends the next year without going "over twenty-four hours without getting high in secret" (p. 1052n279).

[2009] **Year of the Depend Adult Undergarment:** *January–February*: "person or persons unknown went around coating selected toothbrushes . . . with what was finally pinpointed as betel-nut extract" (p. 1077n352).

1 April: Canadian/Saudi medical attaché begins watching *Infinite Jest* (p. 37).

30 April: Marathe meets Steeply in the evening above Tucson, Arizona (p. 87).

9 May: Orin phones Hal to tell him "My head is filled with things to say" (p. 32).

May: for "two or three weeks" events from Gately's childhood come "burpling greasily up into memory" (p. 448).

Possibly at this time "after eight months of indescribable psychic cringing" (p. 462), Gately discovers that the "potential Murder-2 investigation of the botched burglary" (p. 463) has been taken over by the Office of Unspecified Services.

August: "Hal's chronic left ankle had been almost the worst it's ever been" (p. 519).

10 August: Steeply's *Moment* article relating Poor Tony Krause's theft of heart in bag (p. 142).

October: Orin under pressure to do interview with *Moment* (p. 48).

Mid-October: Millicent Kent finds a telescoping tripod (p. 121).

22 *October*: Joelle performs last show as Madame Psychosis? (p. 187).

"before Halloween": Lenz begins to use his knife to kill animals (p. 545).

Lyle begins to say that the most advanced level of insight meditation "consisted in sitting in fully awakened contemplation of one's own death" (p. 898).

1 *November*: Orin in Denver (p. 65).

2 *November*: Graham Rader pretends to sneeze on Troeltsch's lunch tray (p. 60—the passage of this cold seems to lead to Wayne's outburst at the end of the book).

3 *November, Tuesday*: Prescriptive Grammar Exam (p. 95), Hal holds B.B. meeting in V.R. 6.

Orin calls Hal to ask "What all do you know about Separatism?" (p. 137).

Troeltsch "has been taken ill" (p. 60).

Helen Steeply interviews Orin (p. 1026n45).

Letters exchanged between Steeply and Marlon Bain (pp. 663–665).

4 *November, Wednesday*: Hal reads *Hamlet* (p. 171), Pemulis buys DMZ off Antitoi brothers (p. 170).

5 *November, Thursday*: Orin suspects he is being followed by men in wheelchairs (p. 244).

6 *November, Friday*: Inter-Academy matches with Port Washington (p. 217).

7 *November, Saturday*: 1412h Orin leaves a message about Emily Dickinson (p. 1005n110).

Hal looks through one of Mario's "shoeboxes of letters and snapshots" (p. 1004n110).

1600h Orin calls Hal about Steeply's questions (p. 1011n110).

8 *November, Sunday*: Interdependence Day. "Joelle van Dyne . . . entered the House just today, 11/8, Interdependence Day" (p. 1025n134).

A.F.R. kill Lucien and Bertraund Antitoi (given that this is the night that Joelle is a "new resident" [p. 475] and Gately has to go out to get them some food).

1400h Eschaton to start (p. 1011n110): Hal "find himself . . . smoking dope in public without even thinking about it" (p. 332).

1930h usual start time for Mario's film/puppet-show.

9 *November, Monday*: "LATE P.M.": Ortho Stice in Rusk's office "well after regular hours" (p. 550).

"2100h" (p. 551) Pemulis walks in on Wayne and Avril (pp. 552–53).

10 *November, Tuesday*: Hal goes to Dr. Zegarelli for "a removal" from the left side of his face (p. 509).

Hal, Pemulis, Axford, and Kittenplan are summoned to see Tavis and an "urologist in an O.N.A.N.T.A. blazer" (p. 527).

11 *November, Wednesday*: at 0450h Joelle and Gately talk into the early morning (p. 531).

A match is ordered between Hal and Stice (p. 651), and Steeply watches accompanied by deLint and Poutrincourt (pp. 673–82).

The "sub-14 male Eschatonites" (p. 666) discover an abandoned fridge in the tunnels below E.T.A. while Hal and Stice play.

Pemulis and Struck research DMZ at B.U. School of Pharmacy (p. 655).

Orin "once again" embraces "Swiss" hand model (p. 655), who is actually Mlle. Luria P (though the technical interview is apparently later [p. 845]).

1810h mealtime at E.T.A. Steeply sits with the prorectors (p. 627), Ingersoll returns in plaster (p. 635).

"First thing after supper" (p. 686) Hal looks for Schtitt to discuss game, and discovers deLint with a huge chart apparently of E.T.A's top players without his name on it.

Mandatory P.M. study period: Hal sits in V.R. 6 watching *The American Century as Seen Through a Brick*, and *Pre-Nuptial Agreement of Heaven and Hell*; parts of *Valuable Coupon Has Been Removed, Death in Scarsdale, Union of Publicly Hidden in Lynn, Various Small Flames*, and *Kinds of Pain; Wave Bye-Bye to the Bureaucrat* twice in a row (pp. 686–89); and with several others watches *Blood Sister: One Tough Nun* (p. 701).

2030h James Struck plagiarizes Geoffrey Day's essay on separatism (pp. 1055n304).

2100 Mario films as he walks around the academy, and then asks Avril about sadness (pp. 755–69).

2109h Lenz does "two, maybe three generous lines of Bing" at the Brookline Young People's Mtg. (p. 555).

0005h "Nuck duo" (p. 611) come for Lenz (p. 610).

12 November, Thursday: 1930h During a tutorial Pemulis is giving Hal, they discuss addiction (pp. 1063n321).

Possibly on this day Pemulis goes to secret drug stash, Schtitt and Mario go for ice cream, and Avril apparently tries to call Steeply (pp. 700–1).

Marathe has interview at Ennet House (given that he drinks later with Gompert after her assault) (p. 729).

Poor Tony leaves Cambridge City Hospital, robs Kate Gompert and Ruth van Cleve "a little after 2200h" (p. 698), and heads for Antitoi Entertainment, where the A.F.R. presumably use him as a test-subject.

c.2212:30–40h Lenz trails two "very-small sized Chinese women" (p. 716).

2224–26h Poor Tony trips van Cleve with a waste barrel (p. 728).

Kate Gompert drinks with a conflicted Marathe in "Ryle's Inman Square Club of Jazz" (p. 775). Marathe evidently decides not to tell the A.F.R. about Joelle's location.

17 November, Tuesday: "just after 0830" Hal comes to Ennet House to find out about NA meetings (p. 785).

"1420h" Pemulis comes down to shower before a game with Freer (p. 1067n324); shortly after "Wayne is insanely holding forth innermost thoughts for public ears" (p. 1072n324).

deLint, Nwangi, and Watson tell Pemulis he can "either finish out the term for credit or . . . can hit the trail" (p. 1075n332).

Hal goes to an "Inner Infant" (p. 800) meeting in Natick, after playing Shaw—from this point on Pemulis is "very scarce" and takes the truck for long periods (p. 852).

Wayne spends the night at St. Elizabeth's "for observation" (p. 899).

19 November, Thursday: Unable to find Joelle (because Marathe lies to them), A.F.R. decide to "acquire members of the immediate family of the *auteur*" (p. 845).

Lenz and Poor Tony watch *Infinite Jest* as part of the A.F.R.'s tests at the Antitoi's (p. 845).

"Otis P. Lord had undergone a procedure for the removal of the Hitachi monitor on Thursday" (p. 948).

(During the night heavy snow begins to fall [p. 851]).

20 November, Friday: Hal wakes "before 0500h" (p. 851).

Pemulis tries to speak to a horizontal Hal about the DMZ (given that there are "twenty days" before urine tests [p. 908]); Stice pulled off window.

Weather-delayed meeting between Tine Snr & Jnr, Maureen Hoolcy, Carl Yee, and Tom Veals takes place about entertainment-warning advert (pp. 876–83).

"IMMEDIATELY PRE-FUNDRAISER" (p. 964): Otis P. Lord "out of post-op" makes an appearance in the changing room (p. 965).

20–21 November: Hal, Pemulis and Axford agree on this date as the window of opportunity for testing the DMZ (p. 217).

Saturday 21 November: "C.T. and Schtitt have arranged a special one-match double's exhibition for the Sat A.M. following the big meet" (p. 217).

28 November: Orin plays the Patriots (p. 1009n110).

29 November: Whataburger.

? November: Hal in emergency room (p. 16).

10 December: Date urine samples are due (29 days after 11 Nov. [p. 635]).

[2010] **Year of Glad:**   "the very last year of O.N.A.N.ite Subsidized Time" (p. 1022n14).

February: Correspondence begins between Tavis and Coach White about Hal being recruited by the University of Arizona (p. 4).

November: Hal waggles during interview at the University of Arizona.

Bibliography

WORKS BY DAVID FOSTER WALLACE

The Broom of the System. 1987. London: Abacus-Little, 1997.

Girl With Curious Hair. New York: Norton, 1989.

"An Interview with David Foster Wallace." With Larry McCaffery. *Review of Contemporary Fiction* 13.2 (1993): pp. 127–50.

Infinite Jest. 1996. London: Abacus-Little, 1997.

"Quo Vadis—Introduction." *Review of Contemporary Fiction.* 16.1 (1996): pp. 7–8.

———. "The Salon Interview: David Foster Wallace." With Laura Miller *Salon* 9 (1996): 42 pars. Online.

A Supposedly Fun Thing I'll Never do Again. Boston: Little, Brown 1997.

Brief Interviews with Hideous Men. Boston: Little, Brown 1999.

"Tense Present: Democracy, English and the Wars over Usage." *Harper's* Apr. 2001: pp. 39–58.

SELECT REVIEWS OF *INFINITE JEST*

Birkerts, Sven. "The Alchemist's Retort." *Atlantic Monthly* Feb. 1996: pp. 106–113.

Brzezinski, Steve. *Antioch Review* 54 (1996): p. 491.

Kakutani, Michiko. "A Country Dying of Laughter. In 1,079 Pages." *New York Times* 13 Feb. 1996: p. B2.

LeClair, Tom. "Radical Realism." *American Book Review* 17.3 (1996): p. 16 + .

McInerney, Jay. "The Year of the Whopper." *New York Times Book Review* 3 Mar. 1996: p. 8.

Moore, Steven. *Review of Contemporary Fiction.* 16.1 (1996): pp. 141–42.

Peck, Dale. "Well, duh." *London Review of Books* 18 July 1996: pp. 14–15.

SECONDARY MATERIALS

Abbott, Edwin A. *Flatland: A Romance of Many Dimensions.* 1884. Introd. Alan Lightman. Harmondsworth: Penguin, 1998.

Borges, Jorge Luis. *A Universal History of Infamy.* Trans. Norman Thomas di Giovanni. Harmondsworth: Penguin, 1973.

Bruni, Frank. "The Grunge American Novel." *New York Times Magazine* 24 March 1996: pp. 38–41.

Budgen, Frank. *James Joyce and the Making of* Ulysses *and Other Writings.* Intro. Clive Hart. London: Oxford University Press, 1972.

Burn, Stephen. "Generational Succession and a Source for the Title of David Foster Wallace's *The Broom of the System.*" *Notes on Contemporary Literature* 33.2 (March 2003): pp. 9–11.

Cioffi, Frank Louis. "'An Anguish Become Thing': Narrative as Performance in David Foster Wallace's *Infinite Jest.*" *Narrative* 8.2 (2000): pp. 161–81.

Cooper, James Fenimore. *The Pathfinder, or, the Inland Sea.* 1840. Intro. Kay Seymour House. Harmondsworth: Penguin, 1989.

Crèvecœur, J. Hector St. John De. *Letters From an American Farmer.* 1782. New York: Dutton, 1957.

DeLillo, Don. *Ratner's Star.* New York: Knopf, 1976.

Dickinson, Emily. *The Letters of Emily Dickinson.* Vol. 3. Cambridge, Mass.: Belknap-Harvard, 1958.

Eggers, Dave. *A Heartbreaking Work of Staggering Genius.* New York: Simon, 2000.

Eliot, T. S. "The Television Habit." Letter. *Times* 20 Dec. 1950: p. 7.

Emerson, Ralph Waldo. *Works of Ralph Waldo Emerson*. Ed. and Intro. J.P. Edinburgh: Nimmo, 1906.

Franzen, Jonathan. "Mr. Difficult." *New Yorker* 30 Sept. 2002: pp. 100–11.

———. "Q. & A.: Having Difficulty with Difficulty." 23 Sept. 2002. *New Yorker: Online Only*. <http://www.newyorker.com/online/content/?020930on_onlineonly01>

Frazer, James George. *The Golden Bough: A Study in Magic and Religion*. Ed. and Intro. Robert Fraser. London: Oxford University Press, 1994.

Gaddis, William. *The Recognitions*. 1955. Intro. William H. Gass. Harmondsworth: Penguin, 1993.

———. *JR*. 1975. Intro. Frederick R. Karl. Harmondsworth: Penguin, 1993.

Hayles, N. Katherine. "The Illusion of Autonomy and the Fact of Recursivity: Virtual Ecologies, Entertainment, and *Infinite Jest*." *New Literary History* 30 (1999): pp. 75–97.

Jacobs, Timothy. "American Touchstone: The Idea of Order in Gerard Manley Hopkins and David Foster Wallace." *Comparative Literature Studies* 38 (2001): pp. 215–231.

Johnson, Steven. *Emergence: The Connected Lives of Ants, Brain, Cities and Software*. London: Lane Penguin, 2001.

Joyce, James. *Ulysses*. 1922. Intro. Declan Kiberd. Harmondsworth: Penguin, 1992.

———. *Finnegans Wake*. 1939. 3rd ed. London: Faber, 1964.

———. *Selected Letters*. Ed. Richard Ellmann. London: Faber, 1975.

Karl, Frederick R. *American Fictions: 1980–2000, Whose America is it Anyway?* Xlibris, 2001.

LeClair, Tom. *The Art of Excess: Mastery in Contemporary American Fiction*. Urbana: University of Illinois Press, 1989.

———. "The Prodigious Fiction of Richard Powers, William Vollmann, and David Foster Wallace." *Critique* 38 (1996): pp. 12–37.

McElroy, Joseph. *Women and Men*. 1987. Normal: Dalkey, 1993.

McHale, Brian. *Postmodernist Fiction*. London: Routledge, 1987.

Melley, Timothy. *Empire of Conspiracy: The Culture of Paranoia in Postwar America*. Ithaca: Cornell University Press, 2000.

Nichols, Catherine. "Dialogizing Postmodern Carnival: David Foster Wallace's *Infinite Jest*." *Critique* 43 (2001): pp. 3–16.

Pynchon, Thomas. *Gravity's Rainbow*. 1973. Harmondsworth: Penguin, 1995.

———. "Is it O.K. to Be a Luddite?" *New York Times Book Review* 28 Oct. 1984: 1+.

Rebein, Robert. *Hicks, Tribes, and Dirty Realists: American Fiction after Postmodernism*. Lexington: University Press of Kentucky, 2001.

Rush, Benjamin. *Selected Writings of Benjamin Rush*. New York: Philosophical Library, 1947.

Smith, Zadie. "What Were You Looking At." *Guardian* Sat. Rev. sec. 16 Dec. 2000: p. 9.

Vollmann, William T. *You Bright and Risen Angels: A Cartoon*. London: Deutsch, 1987.